University of Cambridge

Department of Applied Economics

OCCASIONAL PAPER 19

THE RETURN TO GOLD 1925

The Formulation of Economic Policy
and its Critics

University of Cambridge

Department of Applied Economics

Occasional Papers

The Return to Gold 1925

The Formulation of Economic Policy

and its Critics

by D. E. MOGGRIDGE

CAMBRIDGE

AT THE UNIVERSITY PRESS

1969

PUBLISHED BY

THE SYNDICS OF THE CAMBRIDGE UNIVERSITY PRESS

Bentley House, 200 Euston Road, London N.W.1

American Branch: 32 East 57th Street, New York, N.Y. 10022

© Department of Applied Economics University of Cambridge 1969

Standard Book Number 521 07666 8

Set by E.W.C. Wilkins & Associates Ltd., London, and
printed in Great Britain, at the University Press, Oxford,
by Vivian Ridler, Printer to the University.

Contents

List of Tables

Acknowledgements

This study presents the first results of a larger programme of research into British international monetary policy during the period of the inter-war gold standard.

The period of research which lies behind this paper has been supported, both morally and financially, by many bodies, in particular the Provost and Fellows of King's College, Cambridge, the Master and Fellows of Clare College, Cambridge, the Houblon–Norman Fund, the Canada Council and the Department of Applied Economics. The search for documents found active support from the late Mr. Randolph Churchill, the Bank of England, H.M. Treasury, the Federal Reserve Bank of New York, Mr. P. Sraffa and the staffs of the Marshall Library, Cambridge and of the Public Record Office. Mrs. Silk and her typists in the D.A.E. successfully worked the various drafts into an already heavy schedule.

In the course of completing this study, I have also incurred many intellectual debts. Professors Lord Kahn and Joan Robinson have encouraged me from the start and have provided valuable comments and stimulation. The Director has invariably used his vast store of common sense to improve and refine my thinking. Mr S.V.O. Clarke of the Federal Reserve Bank of New York and Professors R.S. Sayers, I.M. Drummond, Sir Ralph Hawtrey and H.G. Johnson read earlier drafts and provided valuable comments. Any failure to follow so much advice and all remaining faults are, of course, my own.

For permission to cite documents, I would like to thank the following: Lord Kahn (Keynes Papers), the Federal Reserve Bank of New York and the Bank of England (Federal Reserve Bank of New York Archives, Strong Papers), the Controller of Her Majesty's Stationery Office (Public Record Office and Crown Copyright materials), the Chartwell Trust (Chartwell Papers), and Mr. P. Sraffa (Pigou Papers in the Marshall Library of Economics).

Finally, I would like to thank my wife Janet who has seen me through the research, travel, writing and revision stages of this study with unfailing support and good humour and who, with Mr. D.R. Beatty, initially convinced me that I should pursue an earlier interest in this area. If this study is at all intelligible to non-economists (or even to economists) it is largely the result of her persistent criticism, questioning and comments.

D.E. Moggridge

March 1969

Note

Symbols are used in the text to indicate the notes at the foot of the page; numbers indicate the references at the back of the book, starting on page 97

I   Introduction

The decision to return to the gold standard at the pre-war parity of $4.86* announced in the Budget speech of 28 April, 1925 and effective in the exchange market the next day, represents, in many respects, a watershed in British inter-war economic history. After that date, for as long as the Authorities were determined and able to maintain the exchange value of sterling, certain policy options were not open to them, or, in many respects, to their critics. Thus, for example, Keynes, who opposed the return to gold in 1925, shifted his ground after the event and criticised the resulting policies in the light of a fixed exchange rate.[1] Until early August 1931, he did not suggest that the decision be reversed or the exchange rate altered.   This general acceptance of the exchange rate appears most clearly in the Macmillan Report and the Addendum thereto, both signed by Keynes, which rejected devaluation as a solution to current economic problems,[3] and in Keynes' comments at a meeting of the Economic Advisory Council when Ernest Bevin raised the issue:[4]

> 'Mr. BEVIN commented on the fact that, whenever the question of gold was discussed the view was expressed that the process of adjustment must be slow as it depended on the action of foreign countries. For himself, the gold standard was not sacrosanct....Personally, he did not believe it was possible to find a solution of the problem within the four walls of that policy. [the gold standard] ...Would it not be possible, for example, to apply to currency the principle of the sliding scale adopted in wages agreements?

> 'Mr. KEYNES said that he was not himself a strong supporter of the gold standard and that he felt in the end it might be necessary to consider the questions raised by Mr. Bevin. It should, however, be remembered that one of our greatest industries was international banking, which would be hit very hard by such a measure. For this reason, he favoured the adoption in the first place of other expedients that were at once more plausible and less dangerous.'

Or as Tom Johnston, an ex-Labour minister, is said to have remarked after sterling left gold on 21 September, 1931, 'They never told us we could do that.'[5] This general acceptance of the rate, coupled with the existing levels of unemployment, most certainly led to an examination of 'other expedients' or second best solutions.[6] This search had repercussions in 1931 when, although after sterling's fall from gold their adoption became unnecessary, several

---

* The actual parity was $4.86656 or 4.86^{2}\!/_{32}$ but for convenience $4.86 is used in the text as a reasonable approximation.

expedients found adoption and further disrupted the international economy.

The return to gold is also important as a single episode in monetary history whose interpretation, despite several recent biographies,[7] autobiographies,[8] and special studies,[9] is still 'largely composed of the old skins thrown off by the snake of controversy'.[10] The most effective phrases thrown off by the controversialists still dominate our understanding of 1925. They do so largely because until the recent past the history of the event could be written only from secondary sources which included and commented on the controversialists' interpretation of events. True the studies noted above have closed the gap, but their documentation has been partial, if only because the Treasury papers for the period were unavailable,[11] and they have been forced to guess the actual sequence of arguments. This study attempts to rectify these omissions, by dealing with the internal Treasury discussions and soul searchings of the last months before restoration. As such, it provides useful evidence as to both the factors which influenced the decision itself and the style of decision-making that characterised the Treasury of the period.

Debate surrounding the return to gold still largely centres around the particular snakeskin left by J.M. Keynes in his pamphlet *The Economic Consequences of Mr. Churchill.* The controversy centres on two matters: (1) was the decision unwise even at the time with the facts available to those taking it? and (2) why did Mr. Churchill make the decision? Keynes argued that the answer to the first question was yes, because the decision overvalued sterling by a minimum of 10–12 per cent. *[12] This overvaluation meant that the 'awkward problem' of post-war Britain was aggravated by an implicit commitment to a period of deflation.[13] Governor Norman, on the other hand, had different views:[14]

> 'Yes I have made mistakes also. I am now accused for having gone back to the gold standard. It was probably a mistake. And still in those circumstances I should do the same thing again. It is easy to see it afterwards. But a great deal of what has happened in the meantime was not necessary but depended on policy. It might have been different.'

On the second matter, Keynes argued that Churchill had made the decision, 'Partly, perhaps, because he has no instinctive judgement to prevent him from making mistakes; partly because, lacking this instinctive judgement, he was deafened by the clamorous voices of conventional finance; and most of all, because he was gravely misled by his experts.'[15] On this last ground, Keynes suggested that the experts has miscalculated the degree of sterling's overvaluation and underestimated the problems of removing it.[16]

---

* Overvaluation and undervaluation can be used in several senses. In most discussions during the period under consideration, the terms found use in a purchasing-power parity sense. This usage compares relative price levels through time, but very little else. The more modern usage works in terms of policy goals. In either case, an exchange rate is overvalued if it is too high in comparison with the standard of judgement chosen. See below pages 69–76 and Appendix.

Subsequent debates have largely centred on the two problems of over valuation and its adjustment rather than going back to the original problems facing those entrusted with the decision in 1924–25. Thus the literature is full of references to purchasing-power parity calculations, to one dinner party which is undated but which has repeatedly formed the basis for judgements as to Treasury thinking and the nature of the advice Churchill received[17] and to a rather enigmatic Treasury Committee's report,[18] but rarely does one see references to the limitations of any purchasing-power parity calculations in the circumstances or examinations of the thinking of the Treasury, its Committee and the generally interested public on the stabilisation problem. In the discussion that follows, I shall attempt to remedy these biases and to examine the 1925 decision in the context of contemporary events, largely on the basis of internal memoranda and contemporary public statements.

In the course of this study, after setting the stage for the period preceding the decision, I shall outline the discussions that took place in the Bank, the Treasury and the Treasury Committee with a view to sorting out those factors which appear to have influenced the ultimate decision from those which were largely ignored. I shall then attempt to evaluate the decision from the perspectives and information of 1925 and the immediately following years, before coming to conclusions as to its wisdom or folly. As such, this format will allow a complete analysis of the decision itself and provide some insight into the formulation of official economic policy, a subject all too often ignored by economists and others.

The War and Reconstruction

Before beginning a discussion of the events of 1924–25, the decision must be put in a longer perspective. Britain in 1914 had effectively been on the gold standard with the Bank of England's selling price for gold at 77s. 10½d. per standard ounce since Newton had set the price in 1717, with the exception of an interval during and after the Napoleonic Wars. When the post-war decision had been taken to return to gold in 1821, there had been relatively little debate as to the standard or the ultimate exchange rate, only one over the timing of the return.[19] By the 1830s the gold standard had become an article of faith to economists and bankers and so it remained, with slight rumblings in the 1880s, until 1914. Thus a gold standard at the old parity had an extensive history before World War I disturbed the old order.

The outbreak of war in 1914, with increased risks for shipping, and thus higher insurance rates, and the refusal of the Authorities to include gold under the war risks insurance scheme, meant that the gold points became irrelevant as far as shipping gold was concerned. After remaining well above $5.00 to the pound for some weeks in August and September, the exchange returned to more normal levels as the Authorities agreed to pay sterling for gold deposited in Ottawa with the Canadian Minister of Finance and then fell below the pre-war gold export point as resources were increasingly devoted to the war effort and British and

Allied demands for American goods rose and British exports fell off. At the same time, the main Allied currencies depreciated against sterling. In the course of 1915 the exchanges were pegged by official borrowing and intervention with the proceeds, the British Government's pegging of the dollar exchange beginning in August 1915 after the failure of an earlier effort by a committee of London bankers. Ultimately the intervention peg came to be $4.76 $7/_{16}$, and, with an official Defence of the Realm Act prohibition on the melting of gold coin in December 1916* and other controls on foreign transactions, the Authorities settled down for the duration with the gold standard legally intact. The pegging of sterling involved the use of substantial resources, official support totalling $2,021 million between the financial year 1915–16 and the financial year 1918–19 and private support remaining substantial.[20] At the end of the War, however, the question of future exchange policy required a solution.

As a part of its planning for post-war reconstruction, the Government during the last year of the War appointed a number of Committees to examine the problems of the transition from war to peace and to suggest appropriate policies. As a part of this process, the Treasury and the Ministry of Reconstruction in January 1918 appointed a Committee on Currency and Foreign Exchanges after the War, under the Chairmanship of Lord Cunliffe, the Governor of the Bank, 'to consider the various problems which will arise in connection with currency and the foreign exchanges during the period of reconstruction and report upon the steps required to bring about the restoration of normal conditions in due course.'[21] Before presenting its *First Interim Report* in August 1918,[22] the Committee heard evidence from the Bank of England, 'banking and financial experts', commerce and industry.[23] In its *First Interim Report*, the Committee noted with respect to its recommendations for the restoration of conditions necessary for the maintenance of the gold standard at the old parity, 'we are glad to find that there was no difference of opinion among the witnesses who appeared before us as to the vital importance of these matters'.[24] The Bank of England, for whom Norman had provided the underlying memorandum for the evidence 'assumed', as did everyone else, 'without argument that the aim of policy must be to restore the pre-war Gold Standard in essentials.'†[25] Thus the Cunliffe Committee was merely echoing the opinion of its witnesses when it recommended:[26]

> 'In our opinion it is imperative that after the war the conditions necessary to the maintenance of an effective gold standard should be restored without delay. Unless the machinery which long experience has shown to be the only

---

* This would do more to prevent domestic hoarding than exports. A reduction in hoarding would leave more gold in circulation which the Authorities could tap to increase their own reserves. [Morgan Ch. VII (A)]. Thus the legal existence of the gold standard during the War depended, *ceteris paribus*, on the unavailability of insurance coverage which protected the reserves by preventing private arbitrage at the pegged rate.

† Unfortunately the evidence presented to this Committee has never been published and a copy has not yet found its way to the Public Record Office.

effective remedy for an adverse balance of trade and an undue growth of credit is once more brought into play, there will be a grave danger of a progressive credit expansion which will result in a foreign drain of gold menacing the convertibility of our note issue and so jeopardising the international trade position of the country.

'The pre-requisites for the restoration of an effective gold standard are:-

(a) The cessation of Government borrowing as soon as possible after the war... .

(b) The recognised machinery, namely, the raising and making effective of the Bank of England discount rate, which before the war operated to check a foreign drain of gold and the speculative expansion of credit in this country, must be kept in working order. This necessity cannot and should not be evaded....

(c) The issue of fiduciary notes should, as soon as practicable, once more be limited by law, and the present arrangements under which deposits at the Bank of England may be exchanged for legal tender currency without affecting the reserve of the Banking Department should be terminated at the earliest possible moment.'

These recommendations met with general acceptance. *The Economist* welcomed them in a leading article entitled 'Back to Sanity' as 'an eminently sound document'.[27] The Committee's views were echoed in the November 1918 *Report of the Committee on Financial Facilities* which had a majority of industrial and commercial representatives.[28] However, the Cunliffe Committee's recommendations represented more in the way of general goals than short-term policy guidance. The Committee accepted that sterling would be somewhat overvalued at the old parity although it could not indicate the extent of the overvaluation.[29] Similarly, it did not attempt to lay down short-term lines of attack on the problem at the cessation of hostilities.

Thus when the Armistice came on 11 November, 1918, the Authorities lacked a short-term policy that would help in the achievement of long-term goals. The Government hesitated at the Bank of England's suggestion for an immediate attempt to bring sterling to par before the signing of a peace treaty,[30] if only because it feared the effects of a trade depression at the start of peace.[31] Keynes, who was still attached to the Treasury, suggested a programme[32] to his superiors which would have allowed a free export of gold immediately with such exports subject to a duty of 10—15 per cent, the amount by which Keynes believed sterling to be depreciated from its pre-war parity. The scheme would have restored a free gold market, by allowing gold importers negotiable duty rebate certificates for a similar amount of gold exports. The duty itself could not be increased except by Act of Parliament; whereas, it could be reduced at any time by Order-in-Council. Gold would be freely obtainable at the Bank for export 'without questions asked and with no more direct or indirect hindrances than existed before the War'.[33] Such a programme would have restored 'the *natural* forces which regulated the flow of gold before the War' (emphasis in the original) and 'would allow a large part of the mechanism of freedom to come into play without any violent transition from the existing regime'.[34] It would have moved in the direction of the Cunliffe Report in an ingenious manner, but it fell by the wayside in the ensuing discussions. In the interim, the pegging of the exchange at 4.76^{7}/_{16}$ continued.

Eventually, as the cost of pegging the exchange was very high, the Authorities decided to solve the transitional problem in another manner. On 20 March, 1919, official exchange support ceased and on 1 April official regulations under the Defence of the Realm Act prohibited the export of gold. The latter step occurred despite the protests of Cockayne, the Governor, who would have welcomed gold losses and the resulting pressure on financial policy, but it had the unanimous support of other bankers.[35] Norman, at that time the Deputy Governor, appears to have supported the Governor.[36] In the course of the rest of the year restrictions on various current and capital transactions were relaxed, Treasury borrowing on Treasury bills in New York was halted and through a licensing system a semblance of the free London market in gold was restored in September 1919. The administrative regulations were ultimately consolidated in the Gold and Silver (Export Control) Act 1920, which (as is usual in such cases) was due to expire after five years, on 31 December, 1925. Finally, in the course of the rest of 1919 most prices were decontrolled. Thus the Authorities by late 1919 were able to form an accurate impression of the depreciation of sterling which had occurred in the course of wartime inflation and to gauge the task ahead.[37]

However, having formally left the gold standard, the Authorities had as their primary aim a return to gold. As Sir Otto Niemeyer put it, the policy implications were as follows:[38]

> 'If we are to get back to an effective gold standard with a free market for gold, which was the policy of the Cunliffe Committee and of the Committee consisting mainly of representatives of Commerce and Industry on Financial Facilities after the War which reported soon after the date of the first report of the Cunliffe Committee, and which has been and still is the policy of His Majesty's Government, it is certain that there must be some deflation, some fall in the proportion borne between spending power on the one hand measured in terms of pounds sterling, the best indices of which are the figures of legal tender circulation and bank deposits, and on the other hand the output of goods and services.
> ...
> 'If we recognise this, and remember that though the war has made us poorer, it has also won for us our freedom to go forward on our traditional lines of development to new successes, we need not feel unduly depressed.'

However, the amount of deflation necessary for a return to the pre-war parity depended on developments abroad, particularly in the United States, the only country to return to gold quickly after the War. The American exchange, not domestic conditions, became the official index of the Cunliffe policy's success. Any restrictive American actions had to be matched in London for the exchange to remain where it was and when no American restrictive action took place, British policy still had to be restrictive to work the exchange back to par.

At the same time, the Bank of England had to regain control of its own markets to make its policy effective. At the end of the War, Government expenditure was running far ahead of revenue, the 1918–19 deficit totalling 65.5 per cent of total expenditure; the banking system and the public were highly liquid and heavy creditors of the Government; the initiative for interest rate changes lay largely with the Government whose rate for tap Treasury bills served as the corner-stone of the system of market rates; and with almost one-third of the national debt at maturity under five years (almost one-fifth under three months) the problems of refinancing and debt management loomed large. In this situation, the Authorities would have to run very hard to remain in the same place: every mishap would make the task of returning to gold more difficult.[39]

The struggle for control lasted from the end of the War until 1922. During that period the Government's financial policies were sharply reversed, despite the sharp depression that occurred from mid-1920 onwards. Expenditures were reduced by almost 60 per cent while revenues rose by 27 per cent. A deficit of £1,690 million in 1918–19 was transformed into surpluses of £237.9 million in 1920–21, £45.7 million in 1921–22 and £101.5 million in 1922–23.[40] By March 1922, debt under 5 years had fallen from almost a third to just over a fifth of the national debt.[41] The clearing banks' cash reserves were reduced from 14.3 per cent of deposit liabilities in 1919 to 11.7 per cent in 1922, their secondary reserves falling from 27.3 per cent to 25.3 per cent of deposits during the same period.[42] The money supply remained above its 1919 average level, but by December 1922, currency in the hands of the public had fallen by 14 per cent from the levels of April 1920; while bank deposits had fallen by 2 per cent. Non-financial clearings during the same period fell by almost 40 per cent.[43] All of these indices provide clues to the deflationary pressures that characterised the period. Their results appear in the price statistics: by December 1922 the Board of Trade wholesale price index and the Ministry of Labour cost of living index stood at 64.5 and 79.1 per cent respectively of their November 1918 levels and 48.0 and 64.4 per cent respectively of their 1920 peak levels.

By 1922, the Bank of England had also regained control of the market. The December 1919 Treasury Minute limiting the fiduciary issue of currency notes and the Treasury's policy of adding Bank of England notes to the currency note reserve both served to transfer internal expansionary pressures to the Bank's reserve and hence give it motives for action. The reinstitution of the tender system for Treasury bills in April 1922 was even more significant. Prior to 30 April, 1922, Treasury bills had only been available at fixed rates controlled by the Treasury. This fixed tap rate had inhibited independent movements in Bank Rate, for an increase in Bank Rate by itself merely produced a refusal by the market to take up Treasury bills at the old tap rate, a shift to commercial bills and a rise in official borrowing on Ways and Means Advances from the Bank, which was expansionary as it increased the reserves of the banking system. The resumption of tender sales in April, plus the virtual ending of tap sales in July 1922, meant that market rates were once more determined by the total supply of bills in the market as compared to the total supply of funds. As the Bank had the advantages of a new instrument of market control, open market operations in

Treasury bills, and new contacts with market institutions formed by wartime operations,[44] the 1922 decisions, along with the totality of other events which had occurred since 1920, meant that the Bank's operational position was much stronger than pre-war. In the summer of 1922 the Bank began to use this new power by embarking on active open market operations to control the assets of the market, at first in a slightly expansionary direction.

Thus at the end of 1922, with the economy in the doldrums,[45] the exchange at $4.63½ — a far cry from the low of $3.40 in February 1920 — the Authorities were in a position to begin serious consideration of the tactics for a return to par. The cost of the period since the end of the boom in 1920 had been high as the index for non-financial clearings, a reasonable guide to the level of activity, noted above indicates to some extent. Real G.D.P. had fallen by 6 per cent between 1920 and 1922,[46] unemployment stood at 12.6 per cent, money wages had fallen heavily — by almost 40 per cent or an average of 28s. 6d. per week for those affected — although real wages had risen slightly, and 102 million man-days had been lost in industrial disputes.[47] In 1922 consumers' expenditure, in real terms, stood below the level of 1910 and G.D.P. at factor cost in real terms stood at its second lowest level in this century, the lowest being 1921.[48] It was from this level that the final struggle for par ensued. The Bank and the Treasury still regarded the Cunliffe Report as their 'marching orders'.[49]

From mid-1922 onwards, for over a year, domestic considerations took priority over exchange considerations. The series of Bank Rate reductions 'owing to domestic reasons'[50] and the mid-1922 series of open market operations which saw the Bank's holdings of Government securities rise steadily and the market's indebtedness to the Bank fall somewhat are all indications of this orientation. By July, Bank Rate was 1 per cent below the Federal Reserve Bank of New York's discount rate, and even then it was ineffective as market rates fell as low as 1¾ per cent early in July. In August, the market rate was pushed up to 2½ per cent through open market sales, and it remained in this area for several months before falling away in the second quarter of 1923. A deteriorating exchange position, resulting from rising British prices and the final phases of the German inflation which saw funds leaving Europe for America over the sterling exchange brought a rise in Bank Rate to 4 per cent in July 1923, but the new rate was generally ineffective with market rates rising only slightly and remaining close to 3 per cent. The rise occurred despite Treasury opposition.[51] There was some slight pressure on clearing bank reserve ratios, largely through secondary assets, but this was not severe. The situation remained roughly unchanged in spite of the effects on the exchanges of the inflation scare caused by the speech of a Conservative Junior Minister and of the elections which brought the first Labour Government to power. At the end of January 1924 sterling stood at $4.27½ and the gap between U.S. and U.K. prices had widened slightly.

During the period from mid-1922 onwards, although the Cunliffe Committee's goals remained paramount, the Authorities were largely waiting upon events. The Bank was awaiting a settlement of war debts and reparations, uncertainties over which bedevilled the exchanges during the period and affected sterling.[52] British war debts to the United States were settled in February 1923. Other debts, reparations and Central European instability were continual objects of official efforts during this period, but with few results, except in Austria, before the end of 1923.[53] Moreover, both the Bank and the Treasury were expecting the influx of gold into the United States which had occured after 1920 to lead to inflation there which would obviate the need for further British deflation to restore sterling to par.*[54] In the course of 1923 there was considerable discussion of a proposal to accelerate this process by shipping a large amount of gold to America, the sum suggested being £100 million, thus effectively altering the composition of the U.K.'s exchange reserves and incidentally ensuring funds for war debt repayments.[55] The proposal which Niemeyer admitted would 'cause a flutter in the dovecots both here and in America'[56] and which R.G. Hawtrey believed would be 'a very effective substitute for those "great gold discoveries"'[57] was discussed at various intervals and in various forms before November 1923 when Norman finally rejected it as impractical and unlikely to be successful.[58] Just before this, the Committee of Treasury decided that the policy of waiting should continue and that 'any attempt to reconsider the Report of the Cunliffe Committee, at any rate until after a complete settlement of Reparations and inter-allied debts, should be resisted...'.[59] Thus at the beginning of 1924, the Authorities were still determined to wait.

Britain and the International Economy in 1924

By 1924, the United Kingdom was well on the way to recovery from the slump of 1920–22. Manufacturing production which had reached 93.6 in 1920, surpassed that level in 1924 when it reached 100 (1913 = 92.2, 1923 = 90.8).[60] It is true that some industries (chemicals, textiles, shipbuilding, drink and tobacco, miscellaneous metal goods) were producing below their 1920 output level, but generally industries were well above it. All industries, other than coalmining which reflected the drop in coal exports after the Ruhr settlement of almost 18 million tons or double the year over year fall in output, were producing more than in 1923. With the rise in manufacturing output, employment rose. The number of man-years in civil work was 240,000 above the 1923 level, of which 130,000 were in manufacturing (the rises since 1921 were 830,000 and 560,000 respectively).[61] Unemployment, although considerably above the 2.1 per cent average of 1913 for Trade Union members, stood far below the strike-affected June 1921 peak of 20.6 per cent, reaching a low of 7.0 per cent in May.[62] On the basis of the Unemployment Insurance returns, the coverage of which was wider, unemployment had fallen from its May 1921 peak of 2,549,395 or 23.0 per cent of those insured

---

* Gold imports into the United States totalled $1.6 billion between 1920 and 1924. This compares with the total U.S. gold stock at the end of 1924 of $4.2 billion [Federal Reserve Board, *Banking and Monetary Statistics*, (Washington, 1943), Table 156.]

to 1,044,540 or 9.2 per cent in May 1924.[63] Among males, the 1924 levels represented the lowest figures for the decade after December 1920. This unemployment was unevenly distributed among trades. Taking the figures for June 1924, when the overall average was 9.3 per cent,[64] one finds above average percentages in the metal industries, including their suppliers and users other than electrical manufacturing, non-electrical engineering, shipbuilding, textiles, public works contracting, and transport, especially shipping and docking. Given that public works contracting and docking were notorious for the high levels of unemployment associated with their systems of labour hiring, it is significant to note that the high unemployment industries tended to concentrate in the export sector. The lowest unemployment industries, on the other hand, tended towards the domestic market. This distribution of trades also accords roughly with the indications provided by the statistics of industrial production, and existed despite a tendency for the number of workers in the depressed trades to decline. It also coincided with the distribution of wage rates, which tended to remain higher in sheltered trades and had moved against the unsheltered trades since 1920.[65]

This tendency towards divergent patterns of behaviour in the sheltered and unsheltered industries becomes clearer if we compare the 1924 components of G.D.P. with those of 1913, dealing in real terms throughout. Taking 1913 as 100 real G.D.P. in 1924 stood at 91.7, consumer expenditure at 99.5, public consumption at 114.5 and gross fixed capital formation at 132.5. Exports of goods and services, however, stood at 72.0 while imports had reached 100.8.[66] If we compare the behaviour of British exports and imports of goods only with that of world and European exports, the relatively poor British export performance and the high level of imports is more apparent. Again taking 1913 = 100, British exports and imports of goods stood at 75.8 and 103.7 respectively, while the volume of world exports had recovered to 90 and European exports to 74 (both of the latter series including the U.K. figures).[67] Thus even in a period when most of Europe was recovering from the ravages of war-time damage and post-war disorganisation, British exports had done relatively badly.

The problems of British foreign trade in 1924 were highly concentrated in her traditional industries: iron and steel, textiles, coal, shipbuilding and machine tools, although much less so in the last. Steel exports (including under this head iron and semi-manufacturers) in 1924 had reached only 77.5 per cent of their 1913 level; whereas, imports had risen to 104.7 per cent of that base.[68] Similarly, exports of cotton piece goods, which suffered heavily from Indian and Japanese competition in Far Eastern markets, in 1924 stood at only 64.8 per cent of their 1913 level.[69] Coal exports had also fallen off as a result of the slow growth of international trade, increased efficiency in fuel utilisation, the growing use of oil fired ships and competition from other sources of energy, and even the disruption of Ruhr production in 1923 and 1924, which gave a boost to exports, only pushed them to 80 per cent of their 1913 level.[70] Shipbuilding, which felt the effects of world over capacity after the War and of international trade below its 1913 level, found its 1924 output for U.K. citizens or companies at only 80.3 per cent and its exports even lower at 35.2 per cent of their 1913 levels.[71] As this particular group of exports accounted for almost 40 per cent of the value of 1913 exports, its difficulties had a significant impact on the U.K.'s overall post-war export performance.

This rather disappointing export performance, combined with strong import demand had, along with other influences, an important effect on the balance of payments. The change in Britain's overall international position is best seen in Table 1.

Table 1. The current account of the balance of payments of the United Kingdom, 1907, 1911, 1913 and 1924.

Item	1907	1911	1913	1924
Trade Deficit	−137	−152	−146	−337
Invisible Income				
Net Shipping Income	+85	+90	+94	+140
Net Investment Income	+160	+187	+210	+220
Net Short Interest and Commissions	+25	+25	+25	+60
Net Other Invisibles	+10	+10	+10	+15
Excess of Government Overseas				
Expenditure	n.a.	n.a.	n.a.	−25
Balance on Invisibles	+280	+312	+339	+410
Balance on Current Account	+143	+160	+193	+73

n.a. = not available and assumed 0

Source: *Board of Trade Journal.*

In these years as in every year since 1822 the trade balance was in deficit and the income from invisibles was necessary to cover this deficit and allow for short-term lending and long-term foreign investment. Given the pre-war position, any factors tending to increase the deficit on the balance of trade or to decrease the surplus on invisibles would, given the desire and the organisation of the London market to lend abroad, tend to weaken London's international position.

The War transformed London's capital position. Between 1914 and 1919 the cumulative total of transactions on capital account appears roughly as follows:[72]

U.K. Government loans	£1,825 million
Private loans	£260 million
U.K. Government borrowing	£1,340 million
Sales of foreign securities by U.K. Government *	£270 million

* These securities were either requisitioned or purchased by the Government from private holders. They were largely denominated in dollars.

Private sales of securities,
repayments, and net contraction
of London's short-term position   £530 million

The deterioration implied by these transactions is somewhat greater than meets the eye, for, as O.T. Falk observed,[73] the Government loan position made the United Kingdom 'a debtor to strong countries and a creditor of the weak', as the borrowing and security sales were largely American while the lending was largely to France, Russia and Italy and subject to varying degrees of default.* The net effect of these transactions on the current position in any post-war year would be roughly as follows:

(1) The sale of approximately £500 million of privately held securities – £270 million in securities were sold by the American Dollar Securities Committee and private sales were probably as large[74] – would if these yielded 5 per cent on average have reduced the income from overseas investment by about £25 million.[75]

(2) The decline in London's short-term position as either a net or gross creditor[76] from 1913 by approximately £250–£300 million[77] would also have reduced invisible earnings by, say, £5–£10 million. The change in the net short-term credit position and in certain credit instruments also affected the effectiveness of certain instruments of monetary policy as we shall see below.

(3) Government borrowing abroad, combined with the default of governments to which the U.K. was a creditor and the slowness of other debtors to fund their war debt payments, meant that U.K. Government payments abroad rose faster than income. The 1924 deficit of £25 million on Government account as compared to a position of rough balance in 1913 reflects this fact.

The War also meant large merchant shipping losses for the U.K., and in 1924 the tonnage of British registered shipping was almost 700,000 below that of 1914. This too would imply a decline in invisible earnings if utilisation rates remained unchanged.[78]

Given these basically unfavourable influences that operated on the pre-war balance of payments position, even without any other unfavourable events, substantial changes would have been necessary in other items to restore the pre-war position. If any price increases took place, these changes would have had to be more substantial, for with equal changes in export and import prices from their pre-war levels the deterioration in the balance of trade in money terms, assuming no volume changes, would have been substantial owing to the pre-war

---

* The Russian war loans defaulted totalled £423 million (*The Economist*, 'Reparations and War Debts Supplement', 23 January 1932).

deficit position.* Any improvement in the terms of trade would modify this adverse effect. Inflation would also imply some deterioration in the real value of the U.K.'s income from overseas investments as these were predominantly in fixed interest form.[79] Inflation would not affect the income on other invisible items as much, for shipping freights would, to some extent, move with the general price level and short interest and commissions income would reflect price changes in that, with rates unchanged,[80] the same percentage of larger sums resulting from inflation would increase earnings. Thus, even with no changes from pre-war volumes of exports and imports, wartime inflation and changes in the long and short-term capital positions resulting from the War would have implied a deterioration in Britain's international position from that of 1913 or any other typical pre-war year.

The balance of payments estimates for 1924 presented above reflect all of these influences, plus the deterioration in Britain's trading position. The rise in prices since 1913 reflected itself in the net shipping income where the increase of £46 million is almost an exact reflection of the increase in tramp freight rates from 68 in 1913 to 121 in 1924 (1869 = 100)[81] and the decrease in British tonnage. The same influence, plus new overseas issues of £440.3 million between 1920 and 1923, the wartime sales noted above and Russian revolution and other losses of over £150 million,[82] made itself felt in the net investment income which stood £10 million above the 1913 level. The estimate for short interest and commissions reflects inflationary developments, wartime losses, and the twin influences of changing financial instruments and falling commission rates on some parts of London's business. However, the most important change, in many respects, appears at the top of the series, for the increase in the current deficit swamped improvements in the invisibles position in money terms. In real terms the deterioration in both the trade and invisible accounts is striking. The value of the surplus on invisibles in terms of 1913 import prices was £250 million, or £89 million below that of 1913, while the trade deficit at 1913 import and export prices was over £60 million above that of 1913. The deterioration of the U.K. position implicit in these volume changes had been reduced by an improvement in the terms of trade by 25 per cent.[83] Had import and export volumes been unchanged, such an improvement in the terms of trade would have almost eliminated the 1913 import surplus. It was in this light that the 1924 balance of payments position should have disturbed contemporary observers.

Between 1913 and 1924 the balances in particular markets had also changed in a fashion which made the multilateral settlement of the overall British position more difficult. Before the War, Britain had depended on heavy surpluses in her transactions with India, the rest of Asia, Australasia and Africa to cover deficits in Europe and America.[84] Between 1913 and 1924 the trade position between Britain and various groupings of her trading partners changed as outlined in

---

* Although there would be no change in 'real' terms, the change in money terms would be significant given the limited elements in the invisibles account that were inflation-proof.

Table 2.

Table 2.　Bilateral trade balances, 1913 and 1924
　　　　　(£ million)

Area	1913 Balance	1924 Balance	Change
N. and N.E. Europe	−35.8	−65.1	−29.3
W. Europe	−16.9	−29.0	−12.1
Central and S.E. Europe	−21.2	+22.1	+43.3
S. Europe and N. Africa	+6.1	+0.6	−5.6
Turkey and Middle East	−8.5	−22.0	−13.5
Rest of Africa	+19.8	+7.8	−12.0
Asia	+35.7	+31.5	−4.2
U.S.A.	−82.2	−162.6	−80.4
British N. America	−3.2	−35.2	−32.0
West Indies	+0.2	−12.4	−12.6
Central and S. America	−17.2	−61.2	−44.0
Australasia	−8.7	−18.7	−10.0

Source:　B.R. Mitchell and P. Deane, *Abstract of British Historical Statistics*,
　　　　　(Cambridge 1962), Overseas Trade 12.

During this period, the British position deteriorated substantially with respect to
North and North East Europe, the United States, British North America and Latin
America. The only major improvement occurred in Central and South East
Europe where British exports and re-exports to Germany grew although her
imports were halved, thus changing the position from one of a deficit of £19.9
million in 1913 to a surplus of £35.4 million in 1924. This situation could
hardly be stable, as the recovery of German industry and the need of Germany to
export or to reduce her imports to transfer reparations or debt service would tend
to reduce the British bilateral surplus and result in a reversion towards the 1913
position. Within Asia, the Indian surplus had declined from £23.3 to £12.8
million and only increased surpluses with other Asian areas prevented this
greatly affecting the aggregate. However, the key area of deterioration was what
might be called the dollar area, the Americas, where the trade deficit rose by
£156.4 million. When to this deterioration is added the decline in dollar incomes
on invisible account through the sale of dollar securities during the War, war
debts and the shifting of many financial services from London to New York, a
potential source of post 1924 strain becomes immediately apparent. The British
pattern of international settlements and the British balance of payments were
more involved in the American economy and its successful management than

previously, given Britain's need both to minimise her bilateral deficit and to earn sufficient surpluses in third countries.

To these overall changes in the balance of payments and the pattern of settlements, one must finally add changes in the effectiveness of monetary policy between 1913 and 1924–25, for such changes significantly affected Britain's international position. The first major changes involved an alteration in the nature of the short-term securities in the London market. Before the War the sterling bill was supreme as a source of international trade finance. On the other hand, the Treasury bill represented the 'small change' of the London market, the total outstanding in 1913 being no more than 1 per cent of the value of commercial bills outstanding.[85] After the War, changes in methods of trade finance meant that value of commercial bills rarely rose far above the prewar level of £500 million, despite the rise in prices;[86] whereas, the value of Treasury bills outside the Government Departments and the Bank of England stood between £425 and £575 million.[87] Within the class of commercial bills the type of bill predominating changed, for, whereas 60 per cent of the pre-war prime acceptances outstanding were finance bills, after the War the Bank of England discouraged finance bills which became rarer as the Bank was less prepared to discount them.

These changes in the bill market had important effects on monetary policy. First, the factors determining the volume of bills changed. Before 1914 the volume of bills depended largely on the level of business activity and the level of prices; whereas, after the War the volume of bills became heavily dependent on the budgetary position and the debt management policy of the Authorities. Second, the deposit-compelling nature of the volume of bills on London changed. Commercial bills normally carried with them sterling deposits as acceptors had to carry working balances with their London acceptance houses and as the latter had to be in funds to meet acceptances before their due date.[88] The relative decline of the commercial bill meant that the volume of funds automatically in London was reduced. The Treasury bill, by itself, did not compel foreign deposits to come to London. Third, the change in the volume of finance bills affected the effectiveness of Bank Rate and high interest rates. The volume of commercial acceptances in London was relatively inelastic to interest rate changes; whereas, finance bills were very sensitive to such changes.[89] Before 1914, a rise in Bank Rate would induce a reduction in the number of finance bills drawn on London and this, plus the maturing of existing finance bills, gave considerable relief from exchange pressures. After 1918, with the decline of the finance bill, this type of relief from exchange pressure no longer existed and the Bank Rate mechanism depended much more on the attraction of funds from abroad. Thus to achieve a given exchange improvement after the War, the Bank had to pursue a more active policy than previously, for it had to attract much larger deposits rather than rely on the combination of a diminution in the volume of finance bills plus some increase in deposits. True, the Bank's position was somewhat stronger in that the Treasury bill gave it an ideal instrument for open market operations and the connections developed with market institutions during the War increased the areas of consultation and the degree of confidence. However, the larger post-war floating debt and the continual need for official refinancing somewhat reduced the short-term freedom of the Bank to pursue its policy goals, and one must place this loss against the gaining of a new policy instrument by the Bank for use in the changed market conditions of the 1920's.

The second major change in the background factors affecting the conduct of monetary policy lay in the rise of New York as an important international financial centre. This change from a centralised to a decentralised financial system increased the need for foreign balances and foreign exchange transactions for any given volume of business activity. It also complicated London's international position as the sterling—dollar exchange remained the main channel for remittances between New York and areas outside the Western Hemisphere. This meant that changes in the attractiveness of New York as a deposit centre for secondary money markets or changes in New York's volume of lending affected the sterling exchanges independently of the position of the British pattern of settlements and balance of payments at the time. Such exchange changes, under gold standard conditions, would have effects on gold flows which could be troubling to the Authorities, for they could necessitate changes in credit policy unrelated to the balance of payments position. Finally, the existence of a second major money market, where interest rates were much less tied to international than to domestic conditions and where official policies were often likely to be domestically rather than internationally orientated, when combined with the reduction in London's deposit-compelling ability meant that the exchanges were open to potentially greater strains than they had been before 1914. Whether these additional complications would matter to London's policy makers depended largely on the underlying strength of London's position. If it was strong, although the additional strains would make life more complex they would not force frequent conflicts in policy goals; if it was weak, these new strains might prove extremely troublesome.

These changes in the international position of Britain and the associated developments in the domestic economy formed the backdrop against which the 1924—25 discussions concerning the return to gold took place. Most of them had some relevance to the policies actually followed and the exchange rate actually chosen. As to their impact on the participants in 1924—25, an examination of contemporary thought and opinion best tells the story.

II   The Decision to Return

The final series of discussions that led to the decision to return at the pre-war parity in 1925 began just over a year before Churchill took that decision. On 19 March, 1924, Governor Norman drew the attention of his Committee of Treasury* to answers to House of Commons' Questions in which the Chancellor, Philip Snowden, stated that the Government was still guided by the Cunliffe Committee's conclusions as to the desirability of a return to gold at the pre-war parity and that the Government saw advantages in the amalgamation of the Treasury controlled currency note issue with that of the Bank of England. The Committee was then invited to express opinions concerning the desirability of appointing an expert committee to consider the amalgamation of the note issues.[1] The Committee of Treasury must have approved of the idea, for on 16 April Governor Norman wrote to Sir Otto Niemeyer of the Treasury, 'I write to suggest that, if you are in agreement, the Chancellor be asked in the near future to appoint a committee to advise him privately as to the need for amalgamating the Currency Note Issue with that of the Bank, and to propose the terms on which such an amalgamation can be arranged'.[2] Such a committee would almost inevitably bring up the question of the return to gold, for the Cunliffe Committee, which would almost certainly be the point of departure, had recommended that amalgamation await at least a year's experience on the gold standard with a minimum gold reserve of £150 million.[3] Norman went on to suggest the possible membership of such a committee — an ex-Chancellor of the Exchequer as Chairman, Niemeyer, Sir John Bradbury, Sir Basil Blackett, 'an Economist (e.g. Professor Pigou)' and a banker.[4] The matter was discussed with the Chancellor and decided early in May,[5] and invitations went out to the membership which was as follows: Sir Austen Chamberlain (Chairman), Sir John Bradbury, Sir Otto Niemeyer, Professor Pigou and Gaspard Farrer. All the members, except Chamberlain and Niemeyer, had been members of the Cunliffe Committee.

The Deliberations of the Chamberlain–Bradbury Committee, June–October 1924

The Committee met for the first time on 27 June, and before Governor Norman, the Committee's first witness, appeared it discussed its terms of reference

---

* The Committee of Treasury of the Bank of England was the executive committee of the Court of Directors and the main policy-making body in the Bank.

'to consider whether the time has now come to amalgamate the Treasury Note Issue with the Bank of England Note Issue, and, if so, on what terms and conditions the amalgamation should be carried out'.[6] The Chairman opened this discussion by drawing the logical conclusion implicit in the terms of reference, and he[7]

> 'pointed out that the question before the Committee was inseparable from the much larger question of the restoration of a free gold market, which has become very prominent since the publication of the Dawes Report and in view of recent discussion. The Chancellor of the Exchequer would probably desire the Committee to consider this wider question, and to hear evidence from the representatives of all classes affected, for instance the views of industrial as well as of financial experts should be invited'.

If anything, this drawing of a conclusion implicit in the Committee's terms of reference should have been expected by commentators on its final Report. Keynes and Professor Cannan, however, were most surprised at this turn of events, despite the fact that they had both given evidence to the Committee on the larger issue, the return to gold.[8]

At this point Governor Norman appeared before the Committee. Prior to his appearance he had discussed his evidence with his Committee of Treasury and, as Sir Henry Clay records it,[9] he had suggested the immediate amalgamation of the note issues, the deferment of any attempt to settle now the amount of the fiduciary issue and the ending of the prohibition of gold exports with the expiry of the enabling legislation at the end of 1925. However before the Chamberlain–Bradbury Committee, he was to take a slightly different tack on the all-important gold standard question.

He began the discussion by noting that if he had been asked to give evidence three months previously he would have concerned himself solely with the issue of amalgamation, for at that time currency expansion and a lack of domestic monetary control resulting from rising American prices affecting British prices through rising raw material costs were his main concerns. However, these questions had since become 'entirely subsidiary' and the gold standard question had become a 'practical one'.[10] The reasons behind this change in attitude were, according to the Governor, as follows: (1) 'the continued depreciation of the exchange'; (2) 'the shrinking from sterling of which I have experience from many parts of the world'; (3) 'the lack of confidence which we ourselves have and have engendered in others in the future of sterling'; (4) the recent reductions in Federal Reserve discount rates; (5) the restoration and return of other areas to gold or near gold.[11] He noted that although his colleagues were in agreement with him on these factors and on the ultimate goal of a return to gold at the pre-war par, they were 'not all precisely agreed as to the machinery of doing certain of these things'.[12]

Governor Norman then set out his proposals for the restoration of the gold standard.[13]

> 'I think the first thing to do is that you should decide a date on which the export [of gold] should be permitted and I think the next thing to do is to

announce it as a fixed and immutable date beyond all possibility of change and to leave me to work towards it ... . I believe it would appear much more reasonable to the public at large and to the community to fix so long a period as three years, and I believe the result would be no less quickly reached than if you fixed a short period. But I think it is extremely valuable camouflage and appears far more reasonable than to fix a short date. Therefore I do not mind a long date, in fact, I favour it.'

He admitted that it would be possible to reach par before the expiry of the prohibition legislation, but he did not think that an average exchange rise of 1 per cent per month after the Committee reported, assuming here a report in the autumn of 1924, was 'a reasonable proposition to put before the man in the street'.[14] He expected that the mere announcement of a definite policy would cause a rise in the exchange because it would show confidence in the exchange,[15] and he thought that the exchange would probably go to par quickly enough to give the Bank some experience at $4.86 before freeing exports of gold, although he was unsure whether the exchange would stay permanently at par and anticipated that the Bank would 'be very apt to back and fill'.[16] He admitted that the transition would not be easy and that this was one reason for his desire for a period longer than eighteen months.[17] Although the Governor did not think that the return would have 'quasi catastrophic'[18] effects on industry, he thought it would 'lead to higher rates here undoubtedly, and to contraction here undoubtedly'[19] and he expected 'a long period of dear money'.[20] The exact effects of a return would depend on American money rates, on European developments, especially in Germany, and on the reduction in British foreign lending that would be part of the process.[21] The Governor did not look to salvation through a rise in American prices, for, as he put it, 'the Federal Reserve people have complete control of their prices'.[22] Thus there was an element of sacrifice in a return to gold which Norman believed the businessman must make for stability, 'for the good of his business and for his future success'.[23] The exact amount of this sacrifice was uncertain, as it depended on developments elsewhere. Norman could not be specific in his estimates of the necessary price adjustments for a successful restoration, for he did not know what the balance between psychology and price adjustment was in the existing exchange value of sterling and he was unsure of purchasing power parity calculations and whether he 'would really believe such calculations if they were made'.[24] Throughout his evidence, the emphasis was on the need for a target date for the return to gold, for a decision and for the freedom to take the measures necessary to make the announced decision a reality. Time was of the essence only for the decision and a public statement of official intentions.

Norman's evidence was followed on 27 June by that of another Bank of England Director, Sir Charles Addis, a member of the Cunliffe Committee and 'the Bank Director on whose advice Norman relied and whom he used most in his discussions on international co-operation with other centres'.[25] Addis was less prepared to wait for the return to gold. He argued that the Government should announce that the legislation restricting gold exports would not be renewed after 31 December, 1925, and that the Bank then take the steps necessary to make such an announcement a success, using the Government statement as 'the reason, and if necessary the excuse,' for those steps.[26] He believed that any period longer than the 18 months to December 1925, such as that proposed by the Governor, would not be credible and as such would be dangerous.[27] Eighteen months would also be sufficient, in his opinion, to allow some adjustment in contracts and to take some of the sting out of the price falls implicit in the return to parity.[28] The amount of deflation necessary for a successful return to parity was uncertain, for he expected some rise in American prices to reduce the existing gap of 10 per cent between the American and British price levels.* [29] He was not adverse to falling prices as such, so long as changes were not sudden, and he pointed to the experience of 'the latter part of the last century' when 'the trade of this country was never more prosperous, nor were the working people ever better off ...'.[30] Addis saw 'further social disturbances, further strikes and discontent' as more likely to accompany the rising prices that a failure to follow his policy of returning to gold would entail than to accompany a return to gold and a fall in prices.[31] He admitted that an increase in Bank Rate and credit contraction would be necessary to make the statement of policy credible and to increase confidence in its successful outcome, but, as he put it: [32]

> 'admitting a sacrifice even though we may differ as to the amount, even if
> it should be the full amount, I think it would not be too high a price to pay
> for the substantial benefit to the trade of this country and its working
> classes, and also, although I put it last, for the recovery by the City of
> London of its former position as the world's financial centre.'

Thus Addis' evidence differed little from Norman's on the issue of the return to gold, except in matters of timing and of the necessary degree of adjustment. Even in matters of timing the difference was very slight, as Norman expected sterling to be at par long before the transition period was over, thus effectively telescoping the necessary adjustments into a comparable period. The difference, in many ways, was merely a matter of public relations.

The evidence presented by the other witnesses who appeared before the Committee in the course of its meetings in the summer of 1924 can be treated in a much more summary manner. The remaining witnesses divided themselves into three groups: (1) those who were more or less opposed to a return to gold at any time; (2) those who were in favour of a return to gold as soon as possible; and (3) those who favoured an ultimate return to gold at the old parity, but had doubts as to the wisdom of such a policy in the existing circumstances. To the evidence of each of these groups I now turn.

Keynes and McKenna were the only witnesses who appeared before the Committee who could be classed as opposing the return to gold, but there were significant ambiguities in the policy implications of their evidence. Keynes argued that the

---

* This estimate suggests very strongly that Addis' calculations were done
  using wholesale prices, for in June 1924 when sterling was at $4.32 or
  11 per cent below par, British wholesale prices were above American
  wholesale prices by a similar amount. Such purchasing-power parity
  estimates appeared frequently in the discussions, as we shall see.

embargo on gold exports should remain in perpetuity and that both imports and exports of gold should be subject to licences which might be generally available for long periods.[33] Within this context he argued that the goal of monetary policy should be price stability, a policy goal which he noted many people who did not agree with him on longer term objectives supported for the transitional period 'until there has been some final decision as to what our ultimate currency policy is going to be'.[34] He argued that a return to parity at the present time would require 'a drastic credit restriction', that it would raise the prices asked for British exports in terms of foreign currencies so 'that in a great many cases ... our export trade would be absolutely cut from under our feet for the time being', and that it would lower import prices so that 'we should also tend to buy more, and the extent to which we should do that would depend on the confidence in this policy being permanently successful'.[35] He admitted that the fall in import prices would limit the rise in export prices in foreign currency in industries that used large amounts of raw materials, but this relief would be limited and would not obviate the need for a fall in costs, largely wages, of about 12 per cent.* [36]

In the longer term, however, Keynes foresaw problems of an entirely different character. He argued that the pursuance of a policy of price stability would 'almost certainly lead to a restoration of the parity of the sovereign, because I find it very hard to believe that American prices will not rise in time, unless they do improbable things'.[37] In fact, Keynes suggested that American inflation would, if sterling was convertible at the old parity, result in Britain being swamped with gold imports, and that this, plus economy in the use of gold, would lead to inflation.[38] As he desired price stability and wanted to prevent this inflation and as he was worried by American financial instability and the power of New York over the international economy, Keynes was opposed to a return to the gold standard.[39] However, if the Authorities desired to return to gold, he suggested that they retain the embargo until it was made useless by other policies, particularly American inflation, and that they retain the power to close the Mint or lower the price of gold to prevent inflationary pressures from abroad pushing British prices up.[40] However, throughout his evidence, it was clear that from his point of view this was a second best policy.

Reginald McKenna's evidence to the Committee was also somewhat ambiguous. He admitted that his basic goal was stability in the prices of goods and services.[41] He would guide monetary policy solely with regard to the price level and pay no attention to the exchanges.[42] McKenna believed that such a policy would not affect the business of London as a financial centre, as it could look after itself on the basis of its own attractions of size, price and quality of service.[43] However, once he had said this McKenna more or less concluded his evidence against the gold standard as a long term goal of policy, for generally

---

* Keynes, in this case, appears to have been using an implicit purchasing-power parity type of calculation, for in June 1924 the exchange was at 88.8 per cent of par, thus making the amount of appreciation involved in a return to gold at $4.86 of the order of 12 per cent. The focus of his calculation, wage costs, is significant.

he could see few objections to returning to gold at the old parity, if sterling returned to par as the result of external events. He saw three advantages in the gold standard: 'the average man's confidence in a currency when it is convertible into something which he can see or handle', the Imperial interests involved in having most gold production in Empire countries, and the prospect of a repetition of the gently rising prices of 1901–14 which would result if gold found use as a basis for credit and was not sterilised and which would be good for trade.[44] He had no fears of a shortage of gold 'because the output today is very great and on any increase in the value of gold the output would be extended'.[45] The only objections McKenna could find against the gold standard in theory were the costs of supporting the price of a commodity whose output was greater than demand and the unsettled position of war debts. As he put it in conclusion, 'On the whole, therefore, if you could get a conference and if you could get the cost of purchasing gold distributed over the whole world, I should be in favour of reverting to the gold standard.'[46]

However, McKenna was unwilling to force the adjustment in prices necessary to revert to the gold standard through domestic policy. As he put it:[47]

'You can only get back to a gold standard by a rise in prices in the United States relative to our price level. There is no other means of getting back. The notion that you can force down prices here until you get to the level of the United States if they remain constant is a dream ... . The attempt to force prices down when you have a million unemployed is unthinkable ... . You cannot get on the gold standard by any action of the Chancellor of the Exchequer ... . He could cause infinite trouble, unlimited unemployment, immense losses and ruin, but he could not balance his Budget while he was doing it, and he would have to begin again to borrow.'

As he expected American prices to rise, owing to the Federal Reserve's shortage of suitable earning assets to offset the gold inflow, he argued that the Authorities should merely keep British prices stable in the interim.[48] As the Americans had an interest in the United Kingdom's return to gold, he argued that there might be a possibility of obtaining an agreement with the United States on war debts as a condition for returning.[49] What he did not advocate was a deflation in the United Kingdom to achieve parity. Thus McKenna concluded his evidence on the gold standard. As to longer term policy it was rather ambiguous, for although he accepted the Keynesian position he could see little wrong with the gold standard as a system, largely because he expected the general international environment in which it would work to be somewhat inflationary. This same expectation had coloured much of Keynes' evidence to the Committee, and as we shall see it had its effects on the results of the summer's deliberations.

Those who favoured a return to gold in the very near future, Walter Leaf of the Westminster Bank, Sir George Paish and Professor Edwin Cannan, did so for somewhat differing reasons. Some accepted the logical case for a managed currency along Keynesian lines, but thought it impracticable. As Professor Cannan put it, 'I quite agree that managed currency is superior if you get the proper people to manage it under all sorts of circumstances, but I don't think it is practicable for this country at present.'[50] However, among the three there was some disagreement as to the timing of a return in the near future and as to the need and degree of adjustment required. Sir George Paish argued that the embargo should be removed at once.[51] He believed that the exchange would go to par and thought a rise in Bank Rate might be unnecessary to keep it there, although it might be used as insurance. He argued that the balance on current account was favourable and that the need for the embargo no longer existed.[52] In fact, Paish suspected that the embargo was inhibiting the accumulation of gold reserves in the United Kingdom, that its removal would lead to an influx of gold, and that restoration would also lead to an increase in foreign balances.[53] Foreign lending, he thought, provided no problems, even in the short run, for, as he put it, 'We do send the credit in goods and not in gold.'[54] Professor Cannan, although he agreed with Paish on timing, thinking 'that if these things are to be done at all they should be done quickly and get it over', thought that there would be some adjustment strains.[55] He admitted that higher rates for money would be necessary and that there would be unemployment, but as he noted of the former, 'That is a thing we have very often had to put up with in the past, and it has not done any great harm.'[56] The important thing was to make the change quickly and suddenly, for that way he argued you would get over the unemployment 'quickly', although he expected that wage reductions would be more difficult to achieve now that unemployment insurance made the unemployed 'more comfortable nowadays than they used to be' and took pressure off trade unions to accept reductions.[57] Walter Leaf was a more transitional figure, more the McKenna of this group than anything else. He assumed that sterling was under valued at the time and argued for a bold policy, a return to gold 'at the earliest possible moment'.[58] He would pay some regard to the condition of trade in that he 'would not put up the Bank rate to about 10 per cent in order to do it', but he would increase Bank Rate immediately to aid the transition by attracting foreign balances to London on an interest and exchange profit basis and by reducing the volume of foreign lending.[59] He admitted that such a change would not be popular in the City, but he argued that it would not cause a 'calamitous fall' in prices, that many trades would be relieved if prices fell and that a higher exchange would bring lower import costs which would benefit trade.[60] Leaf reported his discussions with the Governor to the Committee, most particularly that Norman believed that a return to gold could be effected with a 5 per cent Bank Rate through a gradual rise in the exchange over a period of several months, and Leaf thought it could be achieved before the expiry of the embargo with Bank Rate at that level.[61] In that generally vague state he left matters, refusing to be any more specific as to timing and procedures. However, he deserves inclusion in this group of witnesses because he favoured a return in the fairly near future, within slightly over a year, and because he was not particularly worried about the effects of a return to gold or policies associated with it on industry.

The remaining witnesses before the Committee, Sir Felix Schuster, Sir W.H.N. Goschen, The Federation of British Industries, Messrs. Goodenough and Currie and Sir Robert Horne, all favoured a return to gold at some 'time in the interests both of the financial position of this country and also for its advantages and benefits to the industry and business of this country',[62] but they believed that 'a British initiative in restoring the gold standard at an early date ... would be premature and inadvisable'.[63] They all accepted that there was a considerable adjustment in prices and costs necessary before the gold standard could be successfully restored and that a return would require very dear money.[64] The necessary adjustments would dislocate trade and increase unemployment, and, as the F.B.I. put it, administer 'a severe check' to exports.[65] Sir Robert Horne went so far as to suggest that the announcement of the Government's intention to return to gold would cause a recession through its effects on expectations.[66] Both Horne and the F.B.I., who were the most pessimistic of this group of witnesses, argued that the necessary wage adjustments a deflationary resumption would require 'would ... seriously increase the difficulty of maintaining industrial peace'[67] and would result in 'turmoil, unrest and strikes'.[68] Witnesses in this group were also uncertain as to whether any deadline for returning to gold that would be credible could be met, and they were also uncertain about future political and economic conditions which would influence the success of any policy determined at the present time.[69] Some of the bankers were not averse to a gradual fall in prices,[70] but as there was a general expectation that American prices would rise they were loath to begin deflation at present. Thus the witnesses as a group were, for somwhat differing reasons, in favour of a 'wait and see' policy for the present with general price stability as the short-term goal. However, if this policy did not produce results, or if, as the F.B.I. put it, 'considerations of high finance might make it so important that we should have to take the risk',[71] the witnesses were prepared to reconsider their views.[72]

This emphasis on waiting, with its normal expectation of rising American prices, that was characteristic of the majority of witnesses appearing before the Committee seems to have had its effects on its members. Thus, on 24 July when the Committee had heard all its witnesses except the F.B.I. and Sir Robert Horne who if anything were more alarmed about the difficulties and costs of deflation than any witnesses other than Keynes and McKenna, Bradbury wrote to Farrer:[73]

> 'I am so far impressed by the views of McKenna and Keynes that it may be wise not to pursue a policy of restoring the dollar exchange to parity at the cost of depressing home prices. The odds are that within the comparatively near future America will allow gold to depreciate to the value of sterling — particularly if she realises that it is the only way by which parity will be restored.
>
> My present feeling is rather in favour of pursuing a credit policy which will aim at keeping the exchanges in the neighbourhood of 4.40 while American prices are steady or falling, and working it back to par when prices rise.
>
> 'I doubt the wisdom — at any rate unless and until we are nearer a general economic settlement than seems likely on present indications — of a cut and dried policy at the moment.
>
> 'These are not, however, "settled conclusions", and I am quite willing to modify them after discussion.'

This letter, with its emphasis on exchange stability and semi-price stability in the short run, seems to have summed up the general feelings of the Committee when it came to the first major discussion of its report early in September, a reworking by Professor Pigou of an early draft by the Secretary.[74]

The Pigou draft accepted that 'as a practical present day policy for this country there is, in our opinion, no alternative comparable with return to the former gold parity of the sovereign'.[75] It then moved on to a discussion of whether this restoration was 'a matter of immediate urgency'[76] and concluded that, although a continuation of the Gold and Silver (Export Control) Act 1920 might affect the prestige of sterling, although there was a risk that sterling might be isolated by the development of a European bloc of countries after the adoption of the Dawes Report and the adoption of a gold exchange standard by Germany and although the Dominions might take action to restore the pre-war gold parity individually, there was 'no immediate and pressing urgency' for a British decision to return to gold at pre-war par even though a return as such was a highly desirable goal of policy.[77] The draft report then went on to consider the three possible means by which the pre-war parity of sterling could be restored: (1) price stability in the United Kingdom while American prices rose, (2) deflation in the United Kingdom sufficient to reduce prices sufficiently to raise the exchange to par, or (3) an immediate removal of the embargo on gold exports which would result in a loss of gold and necessitate the adoption of course (2).[78] The second and third courses of action were separated because the bodies taking the necessary decisions were different in the first instance. The draft admitted that the latter two possibilities would involve a discouragement to industry and a threat to British employment which would be 'undesirable to set in motion if there is a reasonable hope that, within a short time, America will permit of our goal being attained by the first of the three routes ... a route which does not involve any enforced recession of sterling prices'.[79] As an increase in American prices was likely, the draft continued, the goal of the Bank of England should be price stability for the time being, particularly as the contingencies that might make stronger action necessary to preserve the exchange value of sterling, a rise in sterling prices beyond the Bank's control or a fall in American prices due to a change in Federal Reserve policy, were remote.[80] Therefore, the draft concluded, 'for another year, the Government should wait upon events. If at the end of 1925 the dollar has not approximated to parity, deliberate Government action to secure that result may become necessary.'[81]

The other members of the Committee, although generally agreeing with Pigou, found him a bit too hesitant in the longer term. Bradbury, as usual, seems the best at expressing the feelings of the majority:[82]

> 'The general impression ... which ... [Pigou's Draft] leaves in my mind is rather flabby. "For the moment we propose to wait and see which way the cat jumps. If she jumps one way, and we can avoid jumping after her — and whether we can or not remains to be seen — everything will probably be all right. If it isn't, we shall be prepared to be a good deal braver than we are at the moment".

> 'I think that we ought to make it perfectly clear that we regard a return to a free gold market at the pre-war parity without long delay as of vital

importance, but that as it involves either a fall in sterling prices or a rise in gold prices, and as there are indications that a rise in gold prices may be imminent, we think it better to wait for a short time and see whether gold adjusts itself to sterling before taking the steps necessary to adjust sterling to gold, but that we do not propose to wait indefinitely, and if our expectations in regard to American prices are not realised in the near future, we shall be forced to adopt the other alternative.

'I would at the same time lay rather more stress than is laid in the draft report as it stands on the importance during this interim period of holding fast to the improvement of sterling which has already been effected, and in particular the necessity of extreme caution in regard to new foreign investments ... I believe there is a real risk that the success of the policy we recommend may be jeopardized by excessive foreign lending ... .'

Farrer and Chamberlain also wanted to take a somewhat stronger line than the draft,[83] and even Pigou was not averse to stronger measures, for as he wrote the Secretary to the Committee in the covering letter to his draft:[84]

'On the main issue, which is one of practical politics rather than economics, whether the Government should take the plunge now or denounce no renewal of the embargo, I am only *just* on balance in favour of a "wait and see" policy. It would be very inappropriate for me as an academic person to *press* for heroism; but if the rest of the Committee had been in favour of it, I doubt if I should have opposed.' (emphasis in the original)

Thus a marginally more emphatic draft resulted, 'B. in P.' as Chamberlain called it,[85] and this draft was sent to the Governor and discussed with him early in October.[86] In it the Committee accepted that sterling could be forced to par immediately and that it was strong enough in an underlying sense to allow a successful return to gold.[87] However, given the necessity of adjusting sterling prices to gold prices by closing a gap of 10–12 per cent and given the domestic 'inconveniences' of deflation, the Committee suggested that the Government wait for up to twelve months for a rise in American prices to reduce the gap while maintaining the current value of sterling and restraining excessive foreign lending either selectively or generally.[88] The draft concluded by recommending that the whole situation be reconsidered in the light of the progress made 'not later than the early autumn of 1925'.[89]

But for the fall of the Labour Government in October 1924, this draft would probably have ended the work of the Committee. Although the resulting Report would have been somewhat averse to forcing an immediate return to gold, there was no doubt as to the Committee's ultimate policy goals and as to its preparedness to place the achievement of these goals above any 'inconveniences' to the domestic economy, to use its phrase for the problems of adjustment. However, in the early autumn of 1924, with sterling below $4.50, the members of the Committee were still uncertain as to the timing of the resumption of gold payments and were still waiting upon events.

If the Government had not fallen and had accepted the Committee's Report, expectations of an early return to gold would have been dashed and the ensuing speculative rise in the exchange would have been avoided. Under these circumstances, in the autumn of 1925 when the time came for a fresh consideration of the Report and the issue of a return to gold, sterling might not have risen much above $4.50 and the Authorities would have been faced with the decision whether to force the exchange to par in the ensuing few months before the expiry of the 1920 Act or of renewing the Act. If domestic conditions were prosperous, the Authorities might have been loath deliberately to create 'inconveniences', particularly as deflation would have been politically unpopular, and they might have consented to an extension of the embargo. Once through that barrier, conditions might have been completely different, particularly as France and Belgium might have stabilised their internal situations and as Germany's undervaluation and competitive threat would have become more apparent. In these different conditions, a return to gold at $4.86, involving as it did an appreciation of sterling, might not have been attempted.

Central Bank Attitudes, June–October 1924

Now that we have followed the development of opinion within the Chamberlain Committee which included the Chancellor's most influential advisers on monetary policy other than the Governor of the Bank – Bradbury and Niemeyer – we must turn to the development of central bank opinion on the return to gold. In this area we are fortunate in having the correspondence of Governor Strong of the Federal Reserve Bank of New York, one of Norman's closest international colleagues. Governor Strong had spent part of the spring of 1924 in London with Norman, and their letters thereafter provide some clues as to internal developments.

After Strong had returned to New York from London, he set out his current views on the return to gold and sterling in a long letter to the Secretary of the Treasury, Andrew Mellon, on 27 May. After outlining the theory of purchasing-power parity and its implications, he continued: [90]

> 'At the present time it is probably true that British prices for goods internationally dealt in are as a whole, roughly, in the neighbourhood of 10 per cent above our prices and one of the preliminaries to the re-establishment of gold payment by Great Britain will be to facilitate a gradual readjustment of these price levels *before* monetary reform is undertaken. In other words, this means some small advance in prices here and possibly some small decline in their prices … . They will be to a certain extent fortuitous, but can be facilitated by cooperation between the Bank of England and the Federal Reserve System in the maintaining of lower interest rates in this country and higher interest rates in England so that we will become the world's borrowing market to a greater extent, and London to a lesser extent. The burden of this readjustment must fall more largely upon us than upon them. It will be difficult politically and socially for the British Government and the Bank of England to force a price liquidation in England beyond what they have already experienced in face of the fact that their trade is poor and they have over a million unemployed

people receiving government aid. There will, however, be a period of time during which the Dawes program is being established in Germany and other debt adjustments are being effected within which cooperation between ourselves and the British can do much toward laying the price foundation required for the safe resumption of gold payment by the Bank of England.

'Assuming that all debt adjustments can be effected upon a satisfactory basis and that price levels readjust to the point where the groundwork for the resumption of gold payment encourages belief in its success and permanence, there is still one important step which must be taken in most skilful fashion. Some large private credits must be opened in this country ... in order to steady the rate of exchange and gradually work it to a higher level corresponding to the international price parity, and hold it there, until the time arrives to actually announce a plan of resumption based upon such adequate credits in this country as will insure the final recovery of sterling to par ... .' (emphasis in the original)

In other words, Strong saw the return to gold in Great Britain as a joint operation with the United States easing the necessary adjustments, and he saw the return as something that could be accomplished in the reasonably near future. [91]

The reductions in New York rates by ½ per cent on both 1 May and 12 June were certainly aimed in this direction, although the former saw domestic considerations as a more prominent determinant.[92] However there were limits to this policy as there were suggestions that Strong was too much under Norman's influence and some Anglophobia.[93] Nevertheless, a further reduction of ½ per cent was effected in August.

Norman, for his part, was attempting to raise rates in London,[94] but was having problems, for as he put it, 'it is necessary to find an excuse for raising it and at this moment no excuse is very apparent.'[95] However, he did not share Governor Strong's urgency as to the need to return to parity; he only desired a statement of policy which was clear and final within the next few months.[96] Norman's rate problems were exemplified by the reaction to Walter Leaf's declaration in June in favour of an immediate rise in Bank Rate to 5 per cent and other measures including an explicit announcement of a policy for returning to gold.[97] As Leaf himself put it, 'I am the most unpopular man in the City on account of it.'[98] This declaration may have been a trial balloon, for Leaf told the Chamberlain Committee of discussions with the Governor about rates,[99] but the adverse reaction is of interest if only because the City expected some rise in rates in the autumn to control foreign lending.[100] However, the Governor was able to secure some stiffening of rates through an agreement whereby the clearing banks increased their rates on discount market fixtures.[101] This increase seems to have occurred at the instigation of the Bank of England, for as Norman cabled Strong, 'In order to facilitate the programme we discussed and to avoid immediate increase in our rate we intend to maintain market rate of discount about ½% higher than in recent months as you may have noticed.'[102]

However, as Norman attempted to increase his rates, Strong appears to have become more sceptical as to the effects of that alone. As he wrote to Norman on 9 July:[103]

'Your reliance upon an advance in bank rate to help the exchange has always struck me as somewhat open to question and based upon past experience in a free gold market. Aside from its possible influence upon prices, are not the direct results of importance, usually but three:
(1) A transfer of balances to London. (2) Discount of bills elsewhere (New York). (3) Reduced foreign loans in London.

'As to (1), I apprehend that so long as you are not paying gold and sterling fluctuates over so wide a range, the risks of exchange loss will deter this movement and London balances will remain at a minimum, at least so far as American houses are concerned.

'As to (2), the total cannot be very large in any event, and as to all bills owned by American banks, which are drawn in sterling, they will not be "carried" in London with American funds, to any great extent, again on account of exchange risks.

'As to (3), undoubtedly our market becomes more attractive for foreign loans than it was, but your bankers are too reluctant to forego the business to make this market any permanent relief, and investment funds here will likely demand higher returns still than in the English market. Opportunity for safe and profitable investment here is still the chief factor.

'So on the whole I do not look for any great results until something more fundamental is undertaken than simply an increase in your rate.'

In the same letter he also questioned the effects of a higher Bank Rate on prices except in a rather uncertain fashion over a fairly long period and again emphasised the need for speed in taking advantage of the existing favourable conditions for the consolidation of sterling's position even if the formal return to gold was a matter of months or years. Later in the summer his scepticism went even further and he began to question the strategy which he had outlined to Secretary Mellon in May. He noted the parallelism of American and British price developments during the summer, despite the differences in policy in London and New York, and suggested:[104]

'I have a feeling that our studies have not yet proved conclusively whether a change in relative price levels in your country and ours must be relied upon as the major cause of a return of sterling to parity; or whether we may not have cause and effect reversed and that some thorough-going plan for restoring sterling to par must be relied upon as the means for a readjustment of price levels to purchasing power parity upon the basis of par of exchange.'

Thus Strong's views were moving in the direction of the necessity of an act of *force majeure* to restore sterling to par. In a sense his views paralleled Norman's presentation to the Chamberlain Committee, but they involved much more drastic action and in many ways a reversal of Norman's priorities. In September the Bank of England was still uncertain as to its future policy and future price behaviour, although it saw the need for some decision as the embargo legislation neared the date of renewal and as the fiduciary issue of currency notes threatened the limit set by the Treasury Minute of 1919.[105] However, events in October 1924 and thereafter were to move the two viewpoints together in the direction of Strong's scepticism.

The Pace Quickens, October 1924–January 1925

The defeat of the first Labour Government in the House of Commons on 6 October and the ensuing General Election removed the decision which Norman had expected on gold policy from the realm of immediate possibility.[106] Norman expressed his uncertainty to Strong in the middle of the election campaign as follows: [107]

> 'As a matter of fact our sudden and unexpected political upheaval has come at the very moment when we had planned and expected an official decision about future gold policy ... . As things are, I cannot say how or when our next Government will decide − We must "wait and see".

> 'As a matter of fact, I can only suppose that the decision will be to declare for a free gold market here either at the end of 1925 or at the end of a somewhat later year, say, 1927.'

In the interim, Norman thought that 'it would be neither necessary nor wise for us to take any strong measures'. However, once the policy of the next Government was settled, Norman noted, 'we must get together and devise a plan which will probably need to include some sort of a credit for steadying or holding the rate of exchange when we get into the eighties'. He also indicated his views on the difficulties of preventing sterling prices rising in sympathy with dollar prices, particularly if raw material prices led the price increase, but he did not go as far as Strong had in September as to the implications of this for policy. That would have to await the election results.

The election on 29 October and its resulting overwhelming Conservative majority seems to have revised expectations considerably. The change appears most clearly in Strong's first letter to Norman after the election, that of 4 November:[108]

> 'Your political "upheaval", as I view it, appears to make plans for a strong policy as to the exchange and a return to gold payment much easier than would have been the case had not the Conservative Party had such a sweeping victory and gained such a large majority in Parliament as to indicate the possibility of the new cabinet continuing in power for some time. I frankly did not look for any such development and it has made me wonder whether your natural conservatism in dealing with the problem may not now be somewhat modified ... .

> 'So we must also consider the subject of the relative price levels, concerning which I have always felt that a great deal of nonsense has been written. We may not adequately take into consideration that changes of prices are not always a *cause* of a change in the exchange rate; in fact, it may at times be the case that changes in rates of exchange are themselves the chief influence upon the relation of international prices. I am inclined to

the view that the latter is the case under present conditions when no movement of "inflation" or "deflation" is under way ... .

'I cannot feel that the shock to your business establishment would be any greater as a result of an advance in sterling from 4.50 to 4.87, than that already experienced in recent months in the advance from below 4.30 to 4.50, or the greater shock resulting from the fluctuations which occurred when sterling advanced to above 4.70 and then declined to below 4.30.

'In a general way the situation appears to me to be somewhat as follows :

1. Your program has been facilitated by the movements of our respective money markets, which has caused some return flow of funds to London and has diverted borrowings from the London market to the New York market.

2. The outlook is improved by the adoption of the Dawes Plan, which should eliminate reparation payments, certainly for the next few years, as a seriously disturbing element in the exchange market.

3. Your election gives a greater political certainty than you have enjoyed for some years, and presumably the new cabinet will be sympathetic to a gold program.

4. If business improves, some action will be forced upon you as to currency notes.

5. You must either return to gold payments before the end of next year, or secure legislation extending the period of the embargo.

6. A continuance of lower money rates in New York than in London cannot be expected to continue indefinitely and may end some-time next year.

7. It is illusory to expect price readjustments of themselves to effect a recovery of sterling. Sterling cannot return to par and gold payment cannot be resumed without an act of "force majeure" ... .'

Norman reacted to the change in circumstances in a somwhat similar manner, for on 4 November he was asking his Committee of Treasury to consider the possibility of obtaining a credit in American to steady the exchange if it approached parity.[109] Strong was, about the same time, putting the possibilities of a credit, of say $200 million, to the Governors' Conference of the Federal Reserve System.[110] Thus on both sides of the Atlantic, and seemingly on the foreign exchanges which rose strongly from time of the election,[111] thinking was moving towards a more speedy restoration of the gold standard in England. In these circumstances, Norman first visited the new Chancellor, Winston Churchill, on 7 November, the date of the new Government's formation.

According to Norman's most recent biographer, the Governor, who still privately wished that Snowden had remained Chancellor, 'found Churchill in the receptive and responsive mood of a backward pupil who was willing to be taught'.[112] Certainly Churchill does not seem to have entered the Treasury with any rigid ideas on financial policy or technical matters. However, Churchill appears to have accepted this ignorance and to have approached all problems with an open mind, with the result that, although he depended heavily on his advisers, he required extensive justifications for every step he had to take, and every step he believed that he might take.[113] As Boyle remarks, Churchill 'would clearly have to be carried' to any decision on gold policy.[114] Events were to prove that he was often something of a burden.

No records seem to exist of the discussion on gold policy during his first month in office, but as P.J. Grigg, Churchill's Secretary 'for the more mundane problems of finance and administration', notes, he 'was certainly told soon after his arrival that the Act under which gold payments were suspended would expire with the year 1925, and that he would, therefore, have to face before very long the choice between going back to gold or legislating to stay off it for another period of years'.[115] By 4 December, however, Norman was writing to Niemeyer of his expected journey to New York at the end of the month, and of his plans concerning a credit which 'should probably exceed $300,000,000' to support a return to a free gold market;[116] and by 12 December, Churchill was writing to Stanley Baldwin, the Prime Minister:[117]

> 'The Governor of the Bank will, I hope, have told you this weekend about the imminence of our attempt to re-establish the gold standard, in connection with which he is now going to America. *It will be easy to attain the gold standard, and indeed almost impossible to avoid taking the decision*, but to keep it will require a most strict policy of debt repayment and a high standard of credit. To reach it and have to abandon it would be disastrous.' (emphasis added)

Thus it would seem that by mid-December 1924, both Norman and Churchill had decided in a very general way to consider, at a minimum, a return to gold in the near future. In some ways, Churchill's letter indicates something more definite.

Norman arrived in New York on 28 December, accompanied by Sir Alan Anderson the Deputy Governor-elect. In the ensuing fortnight he canvassed several people — J.P. Morgan and Governor Strong intensively; Secretary Mellon, Governor Crissinger and Vice Governor Platt extensively — about the return to gold, its timing, expectations of economic trends and policy and possibilities of American support. Throughout the emphasis was exploratory, as Norman had made clear at the outset 'that they were not commissioned either by the Government or by the Bank of England to conduct definite negotiations which would result in the resumption of specie payment and the establishment of a free gold market in England, because their Government had not yet, in fact, made any decision on that subject'.[118] Those whom he consulted 'were unhesitating in expressing the view that the time for deciding upon a resumption of gold payment by England had arrived'.[119] Strong expressed this view and assured him that Federal Reserve policy 'would be directed towards stability of prices so far as it was possible for us to influence prices'.[120] However he warned Norman 'that there were three factors in the situation which might operate at times so seriously to their disadvantage that there was in fact a real hazard to be reckoned with before final resumption was attempted'.[121] First, he believed that the volume of new foreign issues in New York in 1924 had been unusual and had esulted from a particular set of conditions which might not be repeated. Any reduction in the volume of lending by New York might strain the sterling exchange. Second, the Governor emphasised that the volume of war and related debt payments to the United States was large and likely to increase and that these payments would have to be provided in some fashion. Third, Strong continued,

'there must be a plain recognition of the fact that in a new country such as ours, with an enthusiastic, energetic, and optimistic population, where enterprise at times was highly stimulated and the returns upon capital much greater than in other countries, there would be times when speculative tendencies would make it necessary for the Federal Reserve Banks to exercise restraint by increased discount rates, and possibly rather high money rates in the market. Should such times arise, domestic considerations would likely outweigh foreign sympathies, and the protection of our own economic situation, forcing us to higher rates, might force them to maintain still higher rates, with some resulting hardship to business, etc.'

Though these matters were noted and discussed at considerable length, they were probably outweighed by Norman's expectations of the results of not returning to the gold standard. As Governor Strong's memorandum put it in the paragraph immediately following that quoted above :

'But Mr. Norman's feelings, which, in fact, are shared by me, indicated that the alternative — failure of resumption of gold payment — being a confession by the British Government that it was impossible to resume, would be followed by a long period of unsettled conditions too serious really to contemplate. It would mean violent fluctuations in the exchanges, with probably progressive deterioration of the values of foreign currencies vis-a-vis the dollar; it would provide an incentive to all of those who were advancing novel ideas for nostrums and expedients other than the gold standard to sell their wares; and incentive to governments at times to undertake various types of paper money expedients and inflation; it might, indeed, result in the United States draining the world of gold with the effect that, after some attempt at some other mechanism for the regulation of credit and prices, some kind of monetary crisis would finally result in ultimate restoration of gold to its former position, but only after a period of hardship and suffering, and possibly some social and political disorder.'

Given these considerations, the Americans were willing to provide credit facilities for $500 million — $200 million from the Federal Reserve System to the Bank of England and $300 million from J.P. Morgan and Co. and their associates to the British Government — to be used as a cushion after the return to gold.

These general understandings and general arrangements were made clear to and were approved by the Directors of the Federal Reserve Bank of New York, the Federal Reserve Board and the Federal Reserve Open Market Committee early in January.[122] Thus in America, by 11 January, 1925, the way was clear for a return to gold. Norman's next task was to obtain a favourable decision at home. On 6 January, while he was in New York, Norman cabled Cecil Lubbock, the Bank's Deputy Governor, as to the general strategy :[123]

'After consultation as arranged following plan is suggested in principle :

1. Prohibition of export of gold should terminate 31st December and free market should be re-established subject to arrangement of necessary details.

2. No announcement should be made before March nor until the revolving credit below mentioned shall have been arranged.

3. In order to maintain exchange and to ensure general confidence in all events revolving credit aggregating $500 million should be arranged forthwith in New York for use of British Government in connection with and in order to moderate export of gold.

4. Use of revolving credit and export of gold would require progressive increases in Bank of England rate.'

The cable then went on to outline the details of the proposed credit arrangements and to authorise the communication in confidence of the plan to the Chancellor. This cable was followed by an explanatory cable which discussed general attitudes in America and commented on particular features of the proposals. In it Norman noted that 'free exports [of gold] might with advantage be established long before 31st December perhaps after announcement in March and arrangement of revolving credits', that the total of $500 million was 'strongly recommended', and that the object of the credit operation was 'simply to give control of Market as far as possible to Central Banks.'[124] These cables in a very real sense triggered off discussion and the discussions of future months stemmed largely from them.

The London reaction was immediate, and largely centred around procedures and timing. Replying on 10 January, Lubbock in a cable drafted mainly by Sir Charles Addis, with Lord Revelstoke concurring immediately and Sir Robert Kindersley somewhat later, argued :[125]

'(1) ... Much doubt is felt as to the wisdom of obtaining a credit in any form especially any credit not exclusively arranged with Central Banks and some of us would feel reluctant to recommend such a course to British Government.

(2) The restoration of the gold standard should follow and not precede the conditions of trade appropriate to the maintenance of a stable exchange.

(3) With reference to actual date to be now fixed it would be a mistake to anticipate a return to the free export of gold before conditions warrant it. The risk would be too great and the consequences of failure too grave for us to recommend it. We ought to be satisfied that the exchange situation is such as to afford reasonable grounds for believing that the parity of exchange having once been reached could be maintained by the natural play of the market force of supply and demand without resort to any artificial aids such as exists but I think it would be unsafe to rely on its permanence until it has been tested by a period of comparatively stable exchange.'

The cable went on to suggest that if the conditions alluded to in (3) existed before 31 December they would be willing to lift the embargo, but that for the present they were only in favour of a statement of intent by the Chancellor at a comparatively early stage. Opposition in the Treasury existed for basically similar reasons. Niemeyer had said as much before Norman's departure for New York, and at this time he objected once again to 'the cushion' as he called it, as did Sir Warren Fisher.[126] There was also potential opposition to the idea of credits in the Chamberlain–Bradbury Committee from Gaspard Farrer who had made his views known before Norman's departure for America.[127] Thus upon his return to London, Governor Norman would have to argue for his New York proposals, and to some extent modify them.

Throughout January the discussions continued with Norman reporting the tone to Strong as 'general agreement in principle but a strange opposition in detail'.[128] The Chamberlain–Bradbury Committee also resumed sittings for discussion purposes and by 26 January it had another Draft Report for the Governor's consideration before he gave further evidence on 28 January, which reflected the rise in the exchange, the change in expectations and Norman's New York conversations.[129] In general, this draft followed the final *Report* of the Committee with very minor alterations.[130] It recommended that the gold export prohibition not be renewed; that this be announced by the Government in the near future; and that in the interim between the announcement and the expiry of the prohibition the Bank of England be given a general license to export gold which should be freely used when sterling was below the gold export point.[131] It was satisfied that this policy could be carried out without foreign assistance, but saw an American credit as useful for confidence purposes against speculation. However, the Committee believed that this credit, if used, should be treated by the Bank as equivalent to losses of its own gold reserves in its effects upon domestic credit.[132] The Committee estimated that the restoration of parity would require an adjustment of about 6 per cent in the general price level, or about 1½ per cent more than would be necessary to maintain the existing rate of exchange of about $4.79,* and argued that the sacrifices necessary to achieve parity were 'comparatively small'.[133] With opinion in this state, the Governor and Sir Charles Addis appeared before the Committee on 28 January.

Norman opened his evidence by referring to the discussions that had taken place at the Bank during the previous few days and by explaining that opinion was somewhat divided on the matter and that Addis had come along to the Committee 'in order that you might be informed of all the aspects of the question.'[134] He then went on to outline the bases for the change in his views since his previous appearance before the Committee, to note that the rise in the dollar exchange had 'certainly modified or altered my views to the extent that while I was then greatly in favour of a return to gold at an early date, but a date which I could not be brave enough to define then, I am now greatly in favour of a return during

---

* The estimates suggest once more that the calculations were made on the basis of wholesale prices within a purchasing-power parity framework, for they accurately reflected the January 1925 situation in this respect.

this year'.[135] He then reconstructed the results of his New York discussions, mentioning the advantages in the existing political situation and American stability – the possibility of a stock exchange boom being 'a minor question' which might change discount rates ½ to 1 per cent – and emphasising the conjuncture of circumstances that made 1925 more favourable for resumption than any time likely in the future.[136] After a review of the international movement towards gold with specific references to South Africa, Australia, Sweden, Holland and Switzerland, he proceeded to suggest that the announcement of the non-renewal of the embargo should not come until after the March change in the American Congress and the arrangement of the credits which he proceeded to outline, i.e. in April with a general licence for gold exports taking effect the day of the announcement.[137] He emphasised that the chief purpose of the credits was to make clear to speculators the determination of the Authorities to maintain the position which they would be taking up and the uselessness of any attempts to break the sterling–dollar exchange.[138] Thus to Norman the chief purpose of the credits would be to create what Niemeyer would later refer to as the shop window effect.[139] The credit, he said, was unconditional. Its amount would be difficult to change as changes would probably induce the Americans to reconsider their position and he wished to 'start with confidence in the operation on the part of our American friends'.[140] The Governor did not expect American speculative balances in London to prove troublesome after resumption as their size was normal and resumption would probably induce an increase in such balances.[141] In fact, he expected that it was 'very likely' that he would face an influx of gold after resumption.[142]

Addis, on the other hand, while agreeing with Norman's ultimate goals could not 'share the argument for urgency'.[143] He did not think that conditions in the United Kingdom had changed materially in the previous six months; he was unsure as to relative price levels; and he believed that a return to gold should follow the achievement of parity on the exchange market.[144] Referring to Norman's proposals as 'this adventure', he argued that the credits, if used, would make the restoration of an equilibrium position more difficult for they would have to be repaid. They would also induce pressures for credit ease in periods of gold loss.[145] He was prepared to return to gold payments on January 1st, 1926, 'God willing ... bar earthquakes' and argued that a sufficiently tight monetary policy would make such a return possible in the underlying sense without the use of credits.[146] Such a commitment could be made public if desired. However, he was opposed to the use of such devices as Norman proposed in all circumstances.

After a few more comments from the Governor, largely about the stability of American foreign lending which Norman believed existed and about the difficulties of preventing British overlending without the gold standard and the clear signal the exchanges provided in such circumstances, the hearings of the Committee ended.[147] After the hearings the Committee prepared its final *Report* which largely followed the Fourth Draft with only minor amendments by Professor Pigou in the section on the necessity for price adjustments which replaced specific estimates* with the phrase 'a fall in the final price level here of a significant, though not very large, amount', and with the excision of a discussion of foreign lending.[148] In this form, the *Report*, which concurred with the final hearings of the Committee in its minimisation of any problems of adjustment, went to the Chancellor on 5 February.

The Treasury Discussions and the Decision to Return, February—March 1925

At this point, discussions moved to the Treasury, for although there were still differences to be resolved at the Bank,[149] the basis for the expected decision had yet to be laid at the Treasury. There is some doubt as to who initiated the Treasury discussions,[150] but they certainly began in earnest with the circulation of a memorandum from the Chancellor to Norman, Niemeyer, Bradbury and Hawtrey which the Treasury files call 'Mr. Churchill's Exercise' and of which Lord Bradbury remarked[†] 'The writer of the memorandum appears to have his spiritual home in the Keynes—McKenna sanctuary but some of the trimmings of his mantle have been furnished by the "Daily Express".'[151]

Churchill opened his memorandum as follows: 'If we are to take the very important step of removing the embargo on gold export, it is essential that we should be prepared to answer any criticisms which may be subsequently made upon our policy. I should like to have set out in writing the counter case to the following argument:-'.[152] He then proceeded to question the return to the gold standard on several grounds:

(1) 'A Gold Reserve and the Gold Standard are in fact survivals of rudimentary and transitional stages in the evolution of finance and credit.' Domestic credit and stability, Churchill suggested, were independent of the gold standard as the greater British than American stability of the previous three years indicated. British credit internationally could be successfully upheld through financial policy and healthy trade.

(2) 'We are now invited to restore the Gold Standard. The United States seems singularly anxious to help us to do this'. He questioned whether British and American interests were parallel for the cost of maintaining the value of gold would then have to be shared by Britain.

(3) He then suggested an alternative course of action, the renunciation of attempts to re-establish the gold standard and the shipping of £100 million

---

* These estimates followed the Fourth Draft Report and suggested that a fall of about 6 per cent in the general price level would be necessary to make the return to gold at $4.86 a success.

† There is no evidence in the Keynes Papers that Keynes had been directly involved in the drafting of this document, although there is some indication of Churchill's familiarity with Keynesian views.

from the Bank of England's gold reserves to pay war debts. Such a course, he argued, would reduce the debt burden, congest the United States with gold and induce a rise in American prices which would be assisted by shipments of Empire gold production. The rise in American prices and the greater American lending that resulted would raise the value of sterling, reduce the cost of further debt payments and improve trade.

(4) He then moved to the wider effects of the proposed return to gold:
> 'The whole question of a return to the Gold Standard must not be dealt with only upon its financial and currency aspects. The merchant, the manufacturer, the workman and the consumer have interests which, though largely common, do not by any means exactly coincide either with each other or with the financial and currency interests. The maintenance of cheap money is a matter of high consequence.'

A rise in Bank Rate, he suggested, would administer 'a very serious check' to trade and employment and would leave the Government open to the accusation that it had 'favoured the special interests of finance at the expense of the special interests of production'. Such a risk would have to be offset by 'very plain and solid advantages'.

(5) Moreover, he suggested, there was no necessity for urgency. Legislation was renewable.* If the management of the previous few years had been successful, why not continue it, particularly when previous management had taken place against a backdrop of three elections, four Governments, five Chancellors and 'the advent of a Socialist Administration to power for the first time'; whereas, the present prospect was for three or four years of political stability.

(6) Finally, he suggested, that if the United States was so in favour of restoration, the Government should hold out in favour of better terms, particularly when some papers suggested that the conditions surrounding restoration would mean a decline in the position of London.
At this point, Churchill concluded:
> 'In setting down these ideas and questionings I do not wish it to be inferred that I have arrived at any conclusions adverse to the re-establishment of the Gold Standard. On the contrary I am ready and anxious to be convinced as far as my limited comprehension of these extremely technical matters will permit. But I expect to receive good and effective answers to the kind of case which I have, largely as an exercise, indicated in this note.'

This memorandum, along with others which arise later, although possibly a statement of belief, more probably represents an example of Churchill's tactic

---

* Given the views of business and many bankers before the Chamberlain–Bradbury Committee it is probably correct to say that, so long as respectable reasons were given, the political difficulties in prolonging the export prohibition would not have been too great, provided the Authorities acted early enough.

of evoking all that could be said on the other side of a particular argument which Lord Salter notes as characteristic.[153] He normally achieved this most effectively when he put the opposing case very strongly or even made accusations of incompetence. In this particular case, the tactic certainly worked successfully, for it brought a series of replies which reveal much of the pattern of expectations that characterised the Chancellor's senior advisers.

Niemeyer submitted two replies, one referring to Churchill's memorandum by paragraphs and another on these and more general matters to which he appended an unsigned copy of the Chamberlain–Bradbury Committee's *Report*.[154] The latter memorandum began by referring to the gold standard decision as 'probably the most important financial decision of the present decade' and by noting that the decision would incur criticism no matter which way it went. Niemeyer then proceeded to note the repeated declarations in favour of a return to gold by previous 'Governments of all political shades' and the current expectations in Europe and America of a forthcoming decision to return. These expectations, Niemeyer noted, were one of the factors – the others being the attraction of higher interest rates, the movement of American and British prices together, the return of refugee capital that had fled in the inflation scare of the autumn of 1923 and the rise in American foreign lending – which had pushed sterling towards parity. To continue the export prohibition would disappoint these expectations and would not continue the present state of affairs:

'It would reverberate throughout a world which has not forgotten the uneasy moments of the winter of 1923; and would be the more convinced that we never meant business about the gold standard because our nerve had failed when the stage was set. The immediate consequence would be a considerable withdrawal of balances and investment (both foreign *and British*) from London; a heavy drop in Exchange; and, to counteract that tendency, a substantial increase in Bank rate. We might very easily reap all the disadvantages which some fear from a return to gold without any of the advantages.

'With the engine thus reversed, no one could foretell when conditions, political, psychological, economic, would be such that the opportunity would occur again. It would certainly be a long time.' (emphasis in the original)

He then proceeded to point out that the supporters of managed currency were few, that they had advocated a rise in Bank Rate some months previously, and that the overwhelming majority of opinion preferred restoration. The only point under discussion at present was the timing of the restoration, or 'whether sacrifices should be made for its restoration and what the extent of those sacrifices should be'.

Niemeyer then proceeded to outline the work and the evolution of attitudes within the Chamberlain–Bradbury Committee, noting its decision at the outset to consider the question of the restoration of the gold standard. He noted its advice in favour of a restoration at an early date, and repeated its arguments on prices, the underlying balance of trade, the threat posed to the sterling bill by widespread restorations elsewhere and the relative ease of returning – 'this *may* involve a temporary increase in Bank rate' (emphasis in the original). He also mentioned the favourable conjuncture of circumstances then existing in politics, American stability and aid, concerted action with other countries and an easier spring restoration aided by the seasonal strength of sterling.

At this point he began to consider objections to a return to gold. He admitted that the United States had an interest in the gold standard and was anxious to see gold maintain its value, but he pointed out that Britain was a large holder of gold and that the Empire was a major gold producer with similar interests. He noted that the appreciation of sterling would increase the real value of British foreign investments that were largely denominated in sterling and increase the real value of war debts owed to the British Government. The restoration of the gold standard would stabilise the exchanges which was in the interests of British export trade, particularly if the major Dominions returned to gold with Germany and America, and which would prevent the replacement of the sterling bill by a bill denominated in a stable currency. The strengthening of the sterling bill would improve the position of London vis-a-vis New York which had deteriorated as a result of the War. The stabilisation of sterling, he argued, would probably force the Latin countries of Europe to stabilise and devalue their currencies, 'a great step in the restoration of Europe for trade and commerce'. He did not see any conflict between finance and industry on the disadvantages of dear money; the difference was 'rather between the long view and the short view. Bankers on the whole take longer views than manufacturers. But the view is of what is good for trade and industry as a whole, on which after all the banks entirely depend, not of what may enable the Bank to bleed its trader.' Finally he turned to the effects of restoration on trade where the most serious arguments against the gold standard, in his opinion, lay. He continued:

'No one would advocate such a return if he believed that in the long run the effect on trade would be adverse.

'In fact everyone upholds the gold standard, because they believe it to be proved by experience to be best for trade. If it is agreed that we must have the gold standard, is it not better to get over any discomforts at once and then proceed on an even keel rather than have the dislocation (if dislocation there be) still before us ?

'No one believes that unemployment can be cured by the dole, and palliatives like road digging. Every party – not least Labour – has preached that unemployment can only be dealt with by radical measures directed to the economic restoration of trade ... . On a long view – and it is only such views that can produce fundamental cures – the gold standard is in direct succession to the main steps towards economic reconstruction ... and is likely to do more for British trade than all the efforts of the Unemployment Committee.'

Governor Norman's reply was much more direct and much less 'analytical'.[155] It consisted of a number of statements referring to specific sections of the Churchill argument. He agreed with Churchill on the importance of financial policy and economic conditions in national credit, but argued that 'good faith' of which gold was the guarantee and liquid reserves of which only gold was internationally acceptable were also necessary and important. He argued that a gold reserve and the gold standard were as necessary, and as dangerous to do without, as a police force and a tax collector. He asserted that there was no alternative to gold 'in the opinion of educated and reasonable men', and continued:

'The only practical question is the Date.

'The pound sterling on which paper Notes are based has advanced greatly because the date of free gold is believed to be at hand.

"The financial reputation of Great Britain" is such that the world believes 1925 means 1925 and Gold in 1925 by Act of Parliament means Gold in 1925 in fact. Any other course means a declining pound.'

He argued that Britain could not object to the American interest in stabilisation on gold, as she had insisted on the same gold standard in the European stabilisations which she had assisted. He accepted that Britain could ship £100 million in gold to America for war debt payment, but he argued that the Americans would successfully sterilise it. In Britain, on the other hand,

'the result of so reducing our Gold Reserves would be psychological as well as financial: our Note-circulation would probably be discredited at home (as happened e.g. in Germany): specie payment would have to be formally suspended: Exchange would fall ... and fall: and the world-centre would shift permanently and completely from London to New York.'

The Governor then turned to the question of the general interest that had been raised by Churchill:

'In connection with a golden 1925, the merchant, manufacturer, workman, etc., should be considered (but not consulted any more than about the design of battleships).

'Cheap money is important because 9 people out of 10 think so: more for psychological than for fundamental reasons ... . The cry of "cheap money" is the Industrialists' big stick and should be treated accordingly.

'The restoration of Free Gold *will* require a high Bank Rate: the Government cannot avoid a decision for or against Restoration: the Chancellor will surely be charged with a sin or ommission or of commission. In the former case (Gold) he will be abused by the ignorant, the gamblers and the antiquated Industrialists; in the latter case (not Gold) he will be abused by the instructed and by posterity.

'Plain and solid advantages can be shown to exist which justify – and seem to require – this sacrifice by the Chancellor. He could hardly assume office with Free Gold in one country and watch half-a-dozen others attain Free Gold ... without his own.' (emphasis in the original)

He admitted that there would be no urgency for a decision if the Act did not expire, but 'the National Credit of this country presupposes that measure of good faith which has gradually induced the whole world to believe that when an

Act expires, it expires'. The prolongation of the Act would 'shatter' the exchanges and not help trade and industry. The managed finance of the previous three years had 'a golden 1925' as its goal and even its success depended on international confidence which allowed the Treasury to borrow foreign balances in London. In any case, he argued a high Bank Rate would be necessary to reduce foreign lending, whether the U.K. returned to gold or not, as 'the present method of so-called persuasion' could not be successful for very long. The Governor concluded by emphasising that the gold standard was 'the best' Governor 'that can be devised for a world that is still human rather than divine' that the redistribution of the gold sterilised in America would present difficultie in future years and produce inflationary pressures which, however, would be a lesser evil than inflation of the recent European variety; and that Londons' relative weakness as a financial centre resulted from the War not from 'a golden 1925' and would be reduced by the gold standard and its experience.

Lord Bradbury's reply was pitched at a more general level, in many ways, than the previous two.[156] While admitting the possibilities of other systems of international settlement, either generally or among like-minded groups of countries, he believed that for the foreseeable future gold would be the ultimate means of settlement. He admitted that 'managed pounds' rather than golden pounds were feasible, for the goal of management just differed from that under a gold standard while the methods remained the same. He emphasised that 'the scientific advocates of the "managed pound"' were not inflationists as were the normal opponents of the gold standard. However, he thought that the substitution of 'managed pounds' for golden pounds would not eliminate the credit cycle in some form. Such a substitution could only reduce disturbances which would otherwise result from fluctuations in the value of gold, and it would only do that 'if the index on which you work contains a smaller margin of error than the amount by which the real value of gold fluctuates'. To secure this advantage, Bradbury thought, the statistics would need substantial improvement. Turning then to the present decision on the restoration of gold, Lord Bradbury admitted that there would be great force in the argument for waiting for a rise in American prices if there was a reasonable probability of this happening and if the gap between American and British prices was appreciable. However as the difference was 'not more than 2% or 3%' there was little advantage and possibly serious disadvantages in waiting, particularly as the lack of any announcement of resumption would cause a depreciation of sterling, a rise in sterling prices and a restriction of credit if only on managed currency grounds. Lord Bradbury then concluded:

> 'It is not unlikely that such restriction would be far more severe than that which would be occasioned by a restoration of the free gold market, more particularly if the latter operations should take place at a time when dollar prices are rising in America. Indeed I should not be at all surprised if very shortly after the restoration of the free gold market a period of cheap money and easy credit becomes necessary to repel an influx of unwanted gold.'

Finally, there was a long involved reply from R.G. Hawtrey.[157] Hawtrey emphasised that the success of managed money had so far occurred during a period of recovery from a slump when cheap money was necessary, and he wondered what reactions there would be to a period of credit restriction that had not been foreshadowed by gold exports. He also emphasised that 'stabilisation of internal prices is only one of the two primary characteristics of a good currency', the other being 'stabilisation of the foreign exchanges'. He continued by arguing that unstable exchanges were particularly damaging to a country such as Britain which acted as a financial centre, lending short to finance the trade of third countries, for the forward exchange market found it more difficult to arrange coverage when, with stable exchanges in the third countries, the exchange risk would be one-sided. The restoration of the sterling bill's predominance, he believed, was in both the national and the international interest. Stability could be achieved technically through stabilisation on sterling, but he argued that this would only be satisfactory if there was no risk of war and the blocking of exchange reserves of those countries which stabilised on sterling. As they would be unlikely to do so, Hawtrey concluded that the only method of international exchange stability was gold, particularly as in other countries the gold standard was an accomplished fact.

Hawtrey then continued to examine the case for a return to gold at the present time, and by the United Kingdom. To him, the fundamental objection to a return to gold was the 'influence of America on the Commodity value or purchasing power of gold'. The present rising trend of American prices was favourable for a return to gold because it did not necessitate deflation in Britain, but, he argued, the attendant risk of an American deflation once Britain had returned might produce a particularly cruel dilemma at present levels of unemployment, for in present conditions, with unemployment still severe, it would be better to let sterling lapse than to raise bank rate to a deterrent level'. However, he considered that such a decision was unlikely for he expected that the American expansion would continue for some time and communicate itself to Britain through a rise in prices and encourage British trade. 'When the turn of the tide comes,' he continued, 'we shall be able to stand a rise in bank rate without trouble.' He also expected American prosperity and foreign lending to prevent any deterioration in the British international position resulting from British overlending or other causes. He admitted that there was, as Keynes had pointed out, a risk of excessive American expansion, but he suggested that this possibility was remote', and that if it materialised gold could be demonetised without any previous preparation. Hawtrey then moved on to discuss the Genoa Resolutions and their provision for co-operation to maintain the gold standard and the purchasing power of gold. These held out the promise of 'the best of both worlds – stable prices and stable exchanges'. They would prevent a general return to gold from being deflationary by encouraging economy of gold for monetary purposes and agreement to hold the purchasing power of gold stable. However he did not really tie them into the current discussions of policy except to suggest an agreement with the Federal Reserve System that it would not contract credit unless a serious inflation threatened the United States and that the United States would not unload her gold reserves on Britain or vice versa.

In fact, Hawtrey made few suggestions as to immediate policy except that 'no *active* measures at all need be taken' (emphasis in the original). He hoped that the exchange would come to par 'of itself', and if it didn't he opposed credit contraction. If it went to par, but there was a subsequent reaction on the exchanges which resulted not from 'a credit expansion here', but rather from 'an adverse balance of payments' or 'a contraction in America', the Authorities should let 'large quantities' of gold go and suspend the fiduciary issue limit of the Bank of England. If these measures were unsuccessful, as 'it would be inadvisable to raise bank rate to a deterrent level or to contract credit to any serious extent', Hawtrey suggested that 'it would be better to let sterling fall to a discount.'

By 6 February, Churchill had read his advisers' replies to 'Mr. Churchill's Exercise' and the Chamberlain—Bradbury Committee's *Report*, noting that the former were 'very able' and that the latter provided 'a solid foundation of argument and authority justifying the action proposed'.[158] However, he still had points that he wished to raise with Niemeyer and the Governor and he desired more information. In particular, he noted the results of a conversation with Mr. Goodenough of Barclay's Bank.[159] Goodenough favoured a return to gold but 'would deprecate decision being "rushed" '. He argued that the pound should be brought to par and held there for some months, perhaps with American support, before a return was attempted. The intervening uncertainty would be no problem as traders could cover their requirements in the forward market. Any announcement in March or even August would be 'precipitate'. Churchill also commented on Reginald McKenna's recent speech to his shareholders which had seemingly supported the gold standard and which had been used as support for the end the Treasury civil servants desired.[160] As he put it:[161]

> 'I read his speeches as being a deliberately weak defense of the Gold policy the only argument for which might in short be stated as a vulgar superstition. I have private confirmation of the opinions I derived from reading his speech. He is personally opposed to the Gold policy and regards it as unnecessary and unwise.'

On 6 February, Churchill also wrote to Sir Austen Chamberlain, enclosing a copy of the Chamberlain—Bradbury Report and asking for his comments. At this point, Churchill noted that 'the matter is one of considerable urgency, and decision on the question of the Gold Standard cannot long be delayed'.[162]

The reactions to these two notes were fairly rapid. Niemeyer, replied to Goodenough's proposals by pointing out that using a cushion to support the exchange before losing gold and raising Bank Rate implied that they would try 'to maintain an artificial exchange with limited means', and that this would encourage speculation and withdrawals of funds, exhaust the credit (if one was available for this purpose), push sterling to $4.00 or less, and require a Bank Rate of 11 per cent or more 'to stop the rot'.[163] He accepted that traders could cover themselves in the forward market, but argued that this merely passed the uncertainty on to bankers and brokers who would object. Moreover, forward cover only affected goods bought and sold; it did not cover the manufacturer who did not know the price of future goods in the market. He concluded by asking what Goodenough would do if sterling failed to rise to par before December or if sterling fell below $4.79 owing to doubt and subsequent profit taking.

Chamberlain's reply to Churchill's request was equally emphatic.[164] He reported that he had read the *Report* with 'profound interest' and 'complete agreement'. After noting his agreement with the Committee's interpretation of its feelings in the autumn of 1924 and its reaction to recent developments on the exchange, he continued:

> 'I feel sure that, if you make your announcement with *decisive confidence* on your own part, the operation will now be found all things considered, an easy one, and that to delay your decision much longer would be to expose you to a serious risk of a renewed fall in sterling. All the world is now expecting us to return to the gold standard, and has become convinced that we can do it. If we do not do it, we shall not stay where we were, but inevitably *start a retrograde movement*.' (emphasis in the original)

Thus he pressed for an immediate announcement of the decision to allow the embargo to lapse and a general licence to export.

On the same day as Chamberlain's letter, an article by Philip Snowden, the former Chancellor, appeared in *The Observer*.[165] In it Snowden referred to the recent rise in the exchange, the forthcoming expiry of the Act enabling the embargo on gold exports and the general expectation of a decision to return to gold at $4.86. He argued that a return to gold was necessary although the maintenance of gold might present some difficulties. These difficulties would be 'small compared with the evils from which the world is suffering as a result of unstable and fluctuating currencies'. The return to gold did not require prior ratification from the trade balance, because 'a stable currency is one of the essentials of a healthy state of trade'. The necessary risks of returning had to be taken, although they could be reduced through co-operation with the United States. This article indicated the breadth of political support for a return to gold which probably made the ultimate decision easier.

However, discussion continued unabated for over a month. During February, Niemeyer, whom Churchill refused to allow to leave him, reported to Leith-Ross, who had gone to a meeting in Geneva in his place, 'Gold is excessively active and very troublesome. None of the witch-doctors see eye to eye and Winston cannot make up his mind from day to day whether he is a gold bug or a pure inflationist.'[166] The discussion covered much the same grounds as before, and thus generally need not be outlined in detail. However, one particular exchange is of interest in that it crystallises the position that the return to gold held in the official pattern of expectations. The exchange occurred over Keynes' article in *The Nation*, 'The Return Towards Gold'.[167] Niemeyer accepted Keynes as 'a serious critic of monetary policy' and he attempted to answer many of the issues raised in the article. He agreed with Keynes that Bank Rate should rise to prevent excessive foreign lending and that under existing conditions such a rise would not harm trade and employment.[168] However, he disagreed with Keynes' plea for a managed currency and his proposals for a well managed return to gold, if the latter was the ultimate policy. Niemeyer did not expect American prices to rise by themselves by enough to produce parity, and he did not believe that even if they did rise by the requisite amount parity would result, and he pointed to the situation eighteen months previously when prices had been equal and the exchange remained below par. He agreed with Keynes that there were dangers in being linked to the United States,[169] but he argued that the dangers of not being so linked were greater given Britain's position as a trading nation and a financial centre, particularly at a time when other countries were returning to gold. He also noted that there would be risks from the United States under any currency system. In conclusion he noted that, 'Mr. Keynes seems to me to contemplate the main alleged disadvantages of a gold policy (rise of bank rate etc.) while depriving himself, in the interests of an unexplored theory of "Managed Currency", of all the advantages.'

Churchill, on reading the article and Niemeyer's comments, reacted somewhat differently. After a few short comments on particular points of Niemeyer's comments, he fastened on Keynes' reference to 'the paradox of unemployment amidst dearth'[170] and continued:[171]

scarcity

'The Treasury have never, it seems to me, faced the profound significance of what Mr. Keynes calls "the paradox of unemployment amidst dearth." The Governor shows himself perfectly happy in the spectacle of Britain possessing the finest credit in the world simultaneously with a million and a quarter unemployed ... . This is the only country in the world where this condition exists. The Treasury and Bank of England policy has been the only policy consistently pursued. It is a terrible responsibility for those who have shaped it, unless they can be sure that there is no connection between the unique British phenomenon of chronic unemployment and the long, resolute consistency of a particular financial policy. I do not know whether France with her financial embarrassments can be said to be worse off than England with her unemployment. At any rate while that unemployment exists, no one is entitled to plume himself on the financial or credit policy which we have pursued.

'It may be of course that you will argue that the unemployment would have been much greater but for the financial policy pursued; that there is no sufficient demand for commodities either internally or externally to require the services of this million and a quarter people; that there is nothing for them but to hang like a millstone round the neck of industry and on the public revenue until they become permanently demoralised. You may be right, but if so, it is one of the most sombre conclusions ever reached. On the other hand I do not pretend to see even "through a glass darkly" how the financial and credit policy of the country could be handled so as to bridge the gap between a dearth of goods and a surplus of labour; and well I realise the danger of experiment to that end. The seas of history are full of famous wrecks. Still if I could see a way, I would far rather follow it than any other. I would rather see Finance less proud and Industry more content.

'You and the Governor have managed this affair. Taken together I expect you know more about it than anyone else in the world. At any rate alone in the world you have had an opportunity over a definite period of years of seeing your policy carried out. That it is a great policy, greatly pursued, I have no doubt. But the fact that this island with its enormous resources is unable to maintain its population is surely a cause for the deepest heartsearching.'

Niemeyer took up these remarks, and his reply is worth quoting at length.[172] After pointing out that some unemployment arose from factors such as 'maladjustment of labour supplies' and European transit conditions and tariffs which reduced trade, he continued:

'I doubt whether credit policy is even a chief cause, and I at any rate would not advocate, still less be "happy" with a credit policy which I thought would produce unemployment ... .

'You can by inflation (a most vicious form of subsidy) enable temporarily, spending power to cope with large quantities of products. But unless you increase the dose continually, there comes a time when having destroyed the credit of the country you can inflate no more, money having ceased to be acceptable as value. Even before this, as your inflated spending creates demand, you have had claims for increased wages, strikes, lock outs etc. I assume it to be admitted that with Germany and Russia before us we do not think plenty can be found on this path.

'If that be admitted, economic employment can only be given to the extent to which commodities can be produced at a price which existing uninflated wealth can pay for them. As the result of war there has been a great decrease in wealth, and there is consequently less effective demand. The only permanent remedy is to recreate the losses of war – really, not merely by manufacturing paper – and what we have to do for this purpose is (1) to stabilise our currency in relation to the main trading currencies of the world, (2) to reconstruct the broken parts of Europe and (3) to encourage thrift and the accumulation of capital for industry. These methods and not doles and palliatives are going to remedy unemployment (at least to the extent to which it was remedied in pre-war days). We are now trying to put the finishing touch to (1). We have done what we can for (2) League Loans, Dawes etc. We do all we can for (3) especially by repaying debt and by encouraging a belief that currency will not lose its value. Other methods may give for a year or so a hectic prosperity (particularly if as in France there are largely devastated regions to mend) but they won't give a permanent cure ... .

'The above is necessarily put in a doctrinaire way. In practice we have to go now slow, now fast. But the root idea I am convinced is right, and the only way to enable this small island bound to buy and sell largely abroad ... ultimately to support its population.'

This idea of the gold standard policy as an employment policy has come up before,[173] and according to P.J. Grigg it was of some importance in the ultimate decision. Certainly this is a part of the drift of the famous dinner party of 17th March, 1925 which Grigg reports and which has been used by some observers to refute parts of Keynes' *Economic Consequences of Mr. Churchill*.[174] Certainly after the event, the gold standard and resulting trends in unemployment were something that Churchill returned to in his discussions with his advisers.[175]

This confession of faith by Niemeyer was, in many ways, the last important pre-restoration internal decision document. Discussions in the Treasury continued after late February on specific questions raised by the Chancellor, but the general question as to policy does not recur. It may have recurred in discussions with the Governor after his return from holiday in March at the time when Norman had expected official consideration of the policy to occur.[176] However, we have very little evidence on these consultations.[177] We only know their result.

The decision* finally came on 20 March. Norman noted the final meetings laconically in his diary entries for 19 and 20 March:[178]

> 'Chancellor for lunch in Downing Street, Gold return to be announced April 6th or 8th. Cushion to be meanwhile arranged by Bank. I warn him of 6% Bank rate next month.

> 'Prime Minister, Chancellor, Austen Chamberlain, Bradbury, Niemeyer at 2.30. Free gold statement to be in Budget about April 28th ... .'

Sir Otto Niemeyer noted the latter meeting more completely:[179]

Note of Government Decisions

'On Friday, the 20th of March, the Prime Minister discussed the question of monetary policy with the Chancellor of the Exchequer, the Secretary of State for Foreign Affairs, the Governor of the Bank of England, Lord Bradbury and Sir Otto Niemeyer. The following conclusions were reached:

1. That the return to the gold standard should be announced as part of the Budget speech.

2. The announcement to take the form of a statement that the power to prohibit exports will not be renewed after December next, and further, that the licences for the export of gold would be given freely, either from the date of this statement or very shortly afterwards: this point to be further discussed with the Bank.

---

* The decision never went to the Cabinet except as a part of the Budget preview. The leading figures throughout, other than Churchill, were Baldwin and Chamberlain. Churchill made reports as to the progress of implementation to Baldwin, as one suspects did Norman. The parallels with the 1957 Bank Rate decision are of interest. (Chartwell Papers, File 18/8, Churchill to Baldwin, 17 April, 1965; Boyle, *op. cit.*, 162, 177–8; R.A. Chapman, Decision Making, (London, 1969), Ch. 4.)

3. That the Bank rate should not be put up contemporaneously with the Budget statement.*

4. That it was desirable to make arrangements for obtaining a credit in America as an extra precaution and that the Governor of the Bank should make enquiries in America accordingly. It was clearly understood that such a credit was not to be used until (1) substantial exports of gold had taken place, and (2) Bank rate had been put up accordingly. The intention of the American credit was that it should be for show and not for use.

5. The Chancellor of the Exchequer undertook to see the Clearing Banks on Monday, the 23rd March, and to endeavour to obtain from them an undertaking that they would use every effort in terms satisfactory to the Chancellor to discourage the use of gold for internal circulation in this country. It was recognised that unless satisfactory assurances could be obtained from the Bankers, it would be necessary to introduce legislation on this point before any announcement with regard to the gold standard was made.'

Implementing the Decision, March–April 1925

From this point onwards, the attention of the Authorities was to be directed to the details of implementation of the basic decisions of the 20th. These details are best considered under three headings : the arrangement of the cushion, the conditions attached to the cushion by the Federal Reserve Bank of New York, and the agreement with the clearing bankers concerning the internal circulation of gold. We shall examine each of these briefly before turning to a general summary and consideration of the factors influencing the decision to return to gold.

As noted above,[180] one of Governor Norman's intentions in his New York trip was to obtain a cushion to maintain the exchange if that became necessary. The credit, he noted, 'should probably exceed $300,000,000' and would not be used 'until a sufficiently large amount of gold has been shipped to America and a sufficiently high rate had been in operation here'.[181] At this early stage, Niemeyer's reaction was very cool.[182] He noted that the Treasury had a 'nest egg' in New York of about $100 million and held Dominion bonds whose coupons were payable in dollars or sterling at par which would probably fetch $50 million. He also noted that legally the Treasury did not have the power to issue fresh obligations of the sort needed and that, as he put it, 'we should have to legislate and explain our fears'. If the Americans were so interested in gold, he continued, 'ought not the U.S. ... to co-operate without requiring us to go to the pawnshop?' Basically he disliked the idea of pegging the exchange and summed up his

---

* However this undertaking by the Governor was to be valid for only one week after the announcement (T172/1499B, Norman to Niemeyer, 21 March, 1925).

attitude in the following: 'Either the emergency will not arise — because either the gold shipment will be enough to save it or you will be allowed to put up your Bank rate high enough — or if it does the cushion will not save us.' The proposal for the cushion was certainly one of the grounds for the opposition in January to the proposals set out by Norman in his cables from New York.
Sir Warren Fisher disliked it because 'neither the gold standard nor anything else is worth having on sufferance of another country', and because it would advertise a lack of faith.[183] Niemeyer continued to dislike it for his previous reasons and for the implication of conditions on its use in Norman's cable, particularly, the one stating that use of the credit would 'require progressive increases in Bank of England rate'.[184] The discussion of these objections continued throughout January, as both Norman's cables to Strong and Addis' evidence to the Chamberlain—Bradbury Committee indicate.[185] The Treasury also remained unsure as to the need for the loan, the availability of the power to borrow and the size of the loan if needed.[186] The critics in the Bank may have been won over in February by the news that 'in the event of a free Market [a certain country] may decide to withdraw in gold London balances of £20/40,000'.[187] However, the Treasury remained unconvinced and Niemeyer summed up the current thinking in a long note to Norman on 16 March which began with the general observation that time increased his dislike for the scheme.[188] If the Bank was prepared to lose up to £100 million in gold before using the cushion, he questioned the usefulness of the idea, for if that much support wouldn't succeed a cushion wouldn't. He admitted that he could see the advantages of having the cushion 'in the shop window to impress speculative holders of sterling', but he feared that political pressure might force its actual use. He still expressed a preference for bonding the debt interest on American war loans and using the freed Treasury resources if support proved necessary, and he was prepared to use any pledged securities or securities borrowed for the purpose on a deposit scheme. If however, the cushion was adopted as policy, he expressed a preference for a smaller sum, for as much as possible to be borrowed by the Bank, and for any commissions on Treasury credits to be waived to save Parliamentary criticism.[189] As we have seen the cushion was accepted in principle at the meeting of 20 March, but the details were left vague.[190] The Governor put the proposal of a smaller credit raised solely by the Bank from Morgans and the Federal Reserve to Strong soon thereafter,[191] but the latter, after consulting J.P. Morgan, expressed a preference for the larger sum and one central bank and one Government market credit, if only to avoid adverse American comment and to make the two transactions appear separate as the Federal Reserve could not lend to foreign governments. Strong was, however, prepared, if necessary, to accept a smaller total with the sum from the Federal Reserve System remaining unchanged to avoid the need for new negotiations with all the Banks in the system.[192] Norman agreed to this suggestion and the total was reduced to $300 million from the $500 million originally proposed.[193] The upshot was that the Treasury's part of the credits was reduced by $200 million. From that point on there remained only the arrangement of the timing of the loans, as this would depend on the enabling legislation which would guarantee the Bank's borrowing in New York and allow the Treasury to borrow. Initially there was some discussion of the

possibility of putting the gold standard arrangements in the Finance Bill, but as that would not become law until July and as the announcement gap was distasteful to all concerned, a special bill for resumption and the necessary borrowing was conceded.[194] From that point, there were no problems, and the Treasury and Bank arranged terms and passed the necessary formal letters without incident.[195]

In January 1925, Strong proposed for Norman's consideration four conditions which would surround the credits : (1) continuity in the management of the Bank for two years, (2) the necessity for Bank of England approval of any change in the fiduciary limit for the currency note issue, (3) control by the Federal Reserve of the credit used at any particular time, and (4) no British Government barriers to gold exports if necessary to repay the credits.[196] The first was purely a matter for the Bank which Norman accepted in February,[197] but the other three required the co-operation of the Treasury for their realisation. The Treasury agreed to the third, which merely ensured that the Federal Reserve retained control of its own market, before the return to gold,[198] and the fourth received formal acceptance when a Treasury Minute passed under the Gold Standard Act 1925 received approval in May.[199] However, the second condition proved impossible to realise in anything but a nominal sense. The Governor proposed the condition to the Treasury the day after the settlement of 'the date for a public announcement of the golden age', as Norman put it,[200] but the Treasury objected to the proposal as it would mean that, given the Treasury Minute of 1919, the removal of gold from the currency note account would imply contraction and as the Bank would not only have to approve of any change in the limit but also to initiate any proposals for change.[201] There were also objections because such a condition would have to be made public and might thus bring further controversy.[202] The Bank waived this requirement from the Treasury and Strong accepted the suggestion that it be dropped.[203] However, to put Strong's mind at rest, Norman arranged to have a sentence added to the Chamberlain–Bradbury Report :* 'As from the date of the announcement [of resumption of gold payment] until such time as the arrangements governing the fiduciary issue can be put on a permanent basis, the existing limitation of that issue should be strictly maintained.'[204] The Government's acceptance of the *Report* in toto with the inclusion of this sentence proved acceptable to Strong.[205] Thus Strong's conditions of January were generally met.

Finally the Chancellor, to carry out the decisions of 20 March, had to arrange

---

* S.V.O. Clarke (*op. cit.*, 84) argues that 'no such recommendation was included in the committee's report'. However, a comparison of the draft copy sent to Strong by Norman with the *Report* as published reveals that the quoted sentence was missing from paragraph 34. Norman wrote to Strong on 20 April that he was still attempting to obtain the inclusion of a sentence of this sort. It was finally added 'after consultation with the Governor and Lord Bradbury' by Niemeyer with the concurrence of committee members (F.R.B.N.Y., Strong Papers, Norman to Strong, 15 and 20 April, 1925; T160/197/F7528, Niemeyer to Pigou, 17 and 23 April, 1925.)

with the clearing banks an undertaking to prevent the internal circulation of gold coin. The Chancellor met the bankers twice after 20 March and attempted to persuade them not to ask for gold coin in exchange for Bank of England notes or currency notes for themselves or their customers and not to hold gold themselves for reserve purposes.[206] The Treasury wanted to avoid the necessity for legislation on this point which it believed would be psychologically bad and controversial, and it wanted to avoid the risk of an internal drain 'in time of crisis (due to a Socialist government)', or resulting from 'demands from the London agents of foreign powers, from the public which is affected by irresponsible newspaper suggestion and from "sound currency" fanatics.'[207] Reginald McKenna opposed such an undertaking at first and wanted legislation suspending gold payment in coin, and the bankers believed that to prevent the internal circulation of coin would be extremely difficult if it remained legal.[208] They were prepared, however, not to hold gold themselves, and after further discussion they agreed for two years from the date of the gold standard legislation's passage not to acquire or hold gold coin or bullion on behalf of customers resident in the United Kingdom or themselves and to hold all gold that came their way in the course of business.[209] However, to cover themselves against backsliders, the Treasury redrafted the relevant section of the Chamberlain—Bradbury *Report* to allow for legislation resulting from its acceptance if that became necessary, and to make compliance by the banks more likely they included in the Gold Standard Act 1925 a provision that made notes convertible into bullion in amounts of approximately 400 fine ounces at a time and that suspended the free convertibility of gold at the Mint.[210]

With the settling of these final details and the successful arrangement with several other countries of a co-ordinated return to gold on the same day,[211] the United Kingdom returned to gold at the pre-war parity at 4.5 p.m. on 28 April, 1925. Before examining the wisdom of the decision, it would be wise to look at the considerations that seem to have proved influential in the final event and the expectations of the Authorities as to the effects of the return, for many of these were dashed by events after the restoration.

A Summary of the Discussions

In dealing in summary with the arguments employed at the time of the return to gold, it is probably best to look at them under four heads : the consideration of alternative policies, of timing, of adjustment mechanisms and difficulties, and of the underlying British international position.

In the discussions prior to the return devaluation never received serious consideration. The Chamberlain—Bradbury Committee dismissed it in all the various drafts of their report, out of hand at first and as unnecessary given the rise of the dollar exchange later.[212] In the Treasury and Bank of England discussions it was not mentioned as a possibility until after the event and after the publication of Keynes' *Economic Consequences of Mr. Churchill* and Sir Josiah Stamp's Addendum to the Coal Court of Inquiry.[213] At that point the alternative was rejected by Niemeyer and Bradbury largely for balance sheet reasons as it would involve writing down the value of international assets or increasing the value of liabilities.* [214] On the other hand, the managed money alternative received somewhat more discussion as it had received considerable publicity through Keynes and McKenna. The Chamberlain–Bradbury Committee, citing 'the overwhelming majority of opinion' presented to them by witnesses, rejected it as not being a 'practical present-day policy for this country'.[215] Even Keynes accepted this decision on their part as 'intelligible'.[216] As noted previously, in discussions with the Chancellor, only Bradbury and Hawtrey attempted to meet the argument of the Keynes–McKenna school, and both rejected it: Bradbury because he didn't believe it was a practicable alternative as an international system for a world of stable exchanges and because he did not believe it would offer greater stability; Hawtrey because he did not believe that the system with its unstable exchanges was in British interests and because, to a certain extent, he believed that he could achieve the same ends with a Genoa-type gold standard.[217] The Treasury summed up its reasons for accepting gold in its Memorandum which accompanied the Gold Standard Bill:[218]

'Whatever its imperfections, gold has for centuries commanded the confidence of the civilised world and has continued to command it. If the gold standard fails to give complete stability, its adoption is nevertheless the most simple and direct method of obtaining a high degree of stability. It is not proved that any other standard would give even as good results. All countries which have successfully restored stability and confidence in their currencies after the disturbances of the last ten years have done so on a gold basis.'

This last sentence leads, of course, to the final factor against management without gold, management with gold being acceptable to some observers,[219] the spectre of the German and other European post-war inflations. As Lord Bradbury put it, 'the Gold Standard was knave proof'.[220] As Niemeyer put it so often in his memoranda during the period, management was synonymous with inflation and all one had to do was point to European experience to prove the evils of that.[221] Everyone accepted that some price fluctuations with changes in the value of gold were inevitable, although in this regard the Genoa proposals which were 'a matter for the future' provided a possible solution.[222] The managed currency proposal was, in the conditions of 1925, really a non-starter which never received serious consideration.[223]

In fact, in 1925 the most important considerations were not rate choice or management criteria but rather matters of timing. Here, as we have seen in our

---

* If one reckons in sterling, the value of international assets denominated in sterling would be unaffected; whereas, those denominated in foreign currencies (including under this head equities whose dividends are based on profits earned in foreign countries) and dollar liabilities would rise. If one reckons in dollars, the position would be reversed and dollar liabilities do not rise. Bradbury made the distinction between bases for reckoning consistently, but Niemeyer did not and thus did some double counting.

discussions of the Chamberlain–Bradbury Committee and the Treasury and Bank discussions, there was some controversy. Much of the debate turned on the importance of expectations, the best season of the year for such a change in policy and the parallel movements abroad towards gold, although the adjustment mechanisms and the difficulties anticipated also played some part. As we have seen, most of the participants laid considerable stress on the importance of the market's expectation that a return to gold would be likely in 1925 and on the difficulties that would arise if that expectation was disappointed.[224] This fear of a reversal in the trend of the exchange if the decision was delayed appears to have been justified, to some extent, for speculation did exist in the autumn of 1924 and in early 1925. Robert Z. Aliber after a thorough study of the events after the autumn of 1924 found that as spot rates appreciated the premium on forward sterling increased or the discount on forward sterling decreased in a manner that would confirm the overtracking hypothesis that speculators were attempting to run their gains.[225] Throughout this period, sterling became increasingly overvalued on the basis of price indices, a fact which would also indicate a speculative movement to some extent.[226] This speculative improvement in the exchange left the Authorities facing a dilemma : they could either ratify the speculative anticipations and stabilise or they could delay stabilisation and face the prospect of a fall in the sterling exchange, as the speculative balances which Keynes estimated at approximately £100 million were withdrawn. If the Authorities were to ratify the speculation, most observers argued that the spring, a period of seasonal strength for sterling, was clearly the easiest period for a decision.[227] In 1925 the parallel movements of currencies abroad to stability and to gold was also of some moment, particularly as South Africa had announced a return for the summer of 1925 and Australia had privately decided the same and only held off in response to British promises of a decision.[228] Thus, to a considerable extent, external pressures and seasonal factors indicated that a decision was likely in 1925. However, official expectations as to the size of the adjustments necessary to make the return to pre-war par a success and the speed and ease of operation of the adjustment mechanism also heightened the pressure towards decision.

Official thinking about the size of the price adjustments necessary for the achievement of parity was very much conditioned by the actual rate of exchange at any moment, for only the additional price adjustment necessary to hold the exchange above the existing rate was often considered as the adjustment resulting from the return to gold. The Chamberlain–Bradbury Committee's *Report* expressed this view when it noted :[229]

> 'The discrepancy between British and American gold prices which existed in September has not, however, disappeared, though it has been reduced. We must still be prepared to face a fall in the final price level here of a significant, though not very large amount, unless it should happen that a corresponding rise takes place in America, if the rate of exchange is to be restored to and held at the pre-war parity.

> 'In present conditions, however, this argument against immediate action has not, in our opinion, great weight. For the adjustment of price levels

required to restore and maintain pre-war parity needs to be only some 1½ per cent. larger than that required to hold the exchange at its present rate. If the adjustment of price levels necessary to this end is long deferred, the exchange will inevitably fall back to the rate justified by the comparative price levels – or below it, since the psychological causes which have operated to force it up will tend to operate in the other direction – and a period of fluctuating values is likely to ensue … . But if … we are prepared to face any price adjustment which may be necessary to maintain the present exchange rate, there is nothing to be said for refusing to accept the very small (1½ per cent.) extra adjustment involved in the re-establishment of an effective gold standard.'

Even if those concerned accepted the need for a price adjustment greater than the minimal additional one stated by the Committee, however, the issue of the amount of adjustment necessary was generally underplayed. The Governor of the Bank regarded purchasing-power parity calculations with suspicion. As he told the Chamberlain–Bradbury Committee:[231]

'Personally I would not know where to turn for such a calculation and I am not sure I would really believe such calculations if they were made because they are very experimental, these calculations, don't you think? … The only way I should try and make a shot at it would be to ask a certain number of people in whose opinions I have confidence, add them together and divide and on the whole I should trust the result.'

Within the Treasury, there was also considerable distrust of such calculations, and on almost every occasion they found use there occurred a qualifying statement to the effect that 'overmuch importance should not … be attached to any arguments based on precise interpretations of these figures'.[231] Nevertheless, as often noted above,[232] purchasing-power parity calculations entered the discussions at several points and had a powerful influence on implicit thinking about the problem throughout the period. When such calculations actually found use, however, the general rule employed was to use figures of wholesale prices for Great Britain and the United States.[233] Such indices generally tended to move with the exchange rate as they contained a heavy emphasis on staple commodities that move in international trade and had a world price.[234] Thus the precise adjustments required for a successful stabilisation tended to be understated.

However, although those concerned tended to underplay the necessary adjustment required in that they probably understated the difference in relative prices and costs, they did recognise the need for some degree of adjustment. However, they were very imprecise as to the time period involved in the adjustment and as to its exact details. Two basic schools of thought seem to have existed in the spring of 1925 as before, those who expected inflation abroad and those who expected deflation at home. Professor Sayers, largely on the basis of the Chamberlain–Bradbury Committee's *Report* and P.J. Grigg's report of the supposedly fateful supper party, denies that the former group which gambled on a rise in American prices existed or was influential in the final decision.[235] The Chamberlain–Bradbury *Report* did mention the possibility of American prices rising to ease the adjustment process, but it did not put too much stress on the possibility. However, the Memorandum that accompanied the Gold Standard Bill clearly entertained a reasonable probability that American prices would rise when it noted:[236]

> 'The best opinion inclines to the view that allowing for the imperfection of the indexes (sic), any variation from purchasing power parity, if it exists at all, is very small.

> 'If this view is correct, it is far from certain that any serious drop in prices will be required here, even supposing any gap, if there is a gap, is not bridged by a *rise* of prices in America ... . Without making any prophecies and disregarding very short-term fluctuations it may be said that the balance of instructed opinion anticipates a rise rather than a fall in gold prices.'
> (emphasis in the original)

Earlier Treasury discussions had also contained some indication that a rise in prices in America was expected. Bradbury's reply to 'Mr. Churchill's Exercise' concluded on the expectation that 'very shortly after the restoration of the free gold market', a period of cheap money to repel gold imports — presumably caused by a rise in prices abroad — would be necessary;[237] and Hawtrey's advocacy of the gold standard in the near future rested entirely on an expectation of rising American prices as he ruled out deflation as a means of adjustment at existing levels of unemployment.[238] Both Norman and Niemeyer, on the other hand, expected relatively stable American prices,[239] although the Governor did mention the danger of gold inflation in many countries in the near future and Niemeyer did include the reference above from the Gold Standard Bill Memorandum in his final pre-debate note to the Chancellor.[240] Thus, while Professor Sayers may be right to some extent, I suspect that, judging from references made to the subject prior to the event, the expectation of some assistance from rising American prices in the easing of the adjustment to gold played a significant role in the presentation of the problem and in the final decision.

Such an expectation, and perhaps a desire to improve the presentation of the policy both to the Chancellor and to the public, might also explain the analyses of the problems of adjustment presented before the return to gold which, if anything, were generally brief and euphemistic. The Governor expected that the return to gold would require a high Bank Rate and some sacrifice, but generally went no further as to how any necessary adjustments would come about.[241] Similarly, Niemeyer referred to the 'discomforts' of return and the 'extra sacrifice' required to restore gold, and he occasionally went further and noted that the return to gold would require reductions in British costs in the short run, but he was not much more specific as to the mechanism.[242] Bradbury and Hawtrey paid very little attention to the adjustment mechanism associated with the return as they both expected the problems to be largely removed by rising American prices. True the former in his comments at that notorious dinner party indicated that there would have to be 'reductions of costs in particular industries' and that over time 'some contraction of the basic industries would have to be faced', but he did not go further and the context of his remarks seems to indicate that these changes would occur over the onger term and resulted from Britain's loss of her industrial lead rather than from the restoration of the gold standard.[243] The

Chamberlain—Bradbury *Report* was equally vague.[244] True, the Chancellor had heard Keynes' and McKenna's discussion of the ten per cent overvaluation of sterling at $4.86, the ensuing references to the need for deflation after restoration with its social dislocation surrounding attempts to reduce wages and costs, and the final comment of McKenna that restoration 'will be hell'.[245] However, with Treasury and Bank opinion so heavily on the other side, it would be difficult to put too much weight on Churchill's exposure to contrary opinions. Perhaps the best explanation for the lack of attention paid to the problems of adjustment came from R.H. Brand several years later when he suggested that, given the reductions in costs that had occurred since 1920, 'It was not apparent that it was going to be so frightfully difficult to get them down another ten per cent.'[246] This faith, plus the belief that the longer term results of the return to gold would increase British trade and employment,[247] probably go far to explain the lack of consideration of the adjustment mechanism and its operation in the pre and early post gold standard restoration periods. Even in the summer of 1925 when both Bradbury and Niemeyer in their discussions of the coal position did indicate that the return to gold did involve reductions in wages and other costs, the emphasis still remained on the 'temporary' nature of the problem of adjustment,[248] even if American prices did not rise to ease its achievement.[249]

Similar to the lack of attention paid to the need for and the mechanism of adjustment in 1925 was the lack of attention paid to the international position of the United Kingdom and the effects of the restoration of the gold standard thereon.* Throughout the period of intense discussion of the subject after January 1925, there was no discussion of the effects of the appreciation of sterling upon the trade account. In fact, the only references to this area of the balance of payments came in Keynes' evidence to the Chamberlain—Bradbury Committee in the summer of 1924 when he noted the adverse effects of the appreciation of sterling on this particular area.[250] Similarly, there were no discussions of the effects of the appreciation on the invisibles position, except for the passing references to the effects of appreciation in improving the balance sheet position of the United Kingdom.[251] There was one study after the event that slightly inflated the Board of Trade's estimates of the 1924 invisibles position, but it certainly did not aid in the ultimate decision process.[252] In fact, the only statement of the position that seems to have appeared before the event came from the Chamberlain—Bradbury *Report*,† which, after noting that Britain's international financial position was 'in some respects less satisfactory than it

---

* This lack of attention is even more striking when one realises that all of the discussions were dollar-centred and ignored the effects of sterling's appreciation vis-a-vis other European currencies. (See below pages 67, 73, 75—76)

† The Committee on Industry and Trade's *Survey of Overseas Markets*, (London 1925), contained a full discussion of Britain's international position in its introduction dated 12 March, 1925. However, there is no evidence that it had any influence on the Treasury's deliberations.

was before the war', and after pointing out that certain special influences — post-war industrial stagnation and trade dislocation and unsettled war debts except in favour of Britain's creditors — had reduced British exports, concluded that: [253]

> 'our existing volume of exports, visible and invisible, together with the income we derive from foreign investments is still undoubtedly sufficient to meet our foreign debts and pay for our necessary imports, and even to supply a moderate balance for new foreign investment.

> 'In these circumstances a free gold market could readily be established and maintained at the pre-war parity, *provided that by control of credit we adjusted the internal purchasing power of the pound to its exchange parity, and restricted our foreign investments to our normal export surplus.'*
> (emphasis added)

Such discussion as occurred before 28 April centred on the capital account of the balance of payments, particularly on the interactions of American lending and the export of capital from Britain. Here, the emphasis was generally on the stability of American foreign lending which it was thought would strengthen the sterling—dollar exchange as it was transferred abroad and reduce the demands on the London Market.[254] When British lending was discussed, the emphasis was placed on the difficulties of preventing overlending without the clear indicators of gold outflows and increases in Bank Rate and on the ease of correcting overlending on the gold standard, although there were occasional references to the elements of habit and established connections which made London borrowing more than a matter of price.[255] Discussions of the short-term position centred on the foreign balances placed in London, and here the discussants generally emphasised that the volume of balances placed for speculation or for higher interest earnings was 'relatively small', that the existing balances would probably grow with stabilisation, and that changes in Bank Rate could handle any short-term problems.[256] The only disturbing possibility in the short-term position might have been an American stock exchange boom and Norman regarded this as a 'minor question' which again could be handled by a change in Bank Rate of ½–1 per cent.[257] In fact, throughout the discussions of the balance of payments, particularly of the capital account, the discussants repeatedly assumed that after adjustment to gold standard conditions had occurred changes in Bank Rate could handle any potential problems without difficulty. The process of adjustment to the higher parity, its effects on the balance of payments and the time period required to effect adjustment received no consideration.

The Decision, the Discussions and the Chancellor

Given the facts and opinions which appear to have gone into the decision, it is possible to sort out the factors which appear to have influenced Churchill to decide in favour of gold at $4.86 in 1925. The Chancellor appears ultimately to have agreed to the decision for four basic reasons. First, any decision not to return to gold at the pre-war parity carried very great political costs, given the

66

unanimity of informed business, financial and political opinion on such matters.[258] In this respect, Keynes and McKenna with all their ambiguities were definitely in the minority. As Sir Frederick Leith-Ross put it, one reason Churchill decided for gold was 'because he knew that if he adopted this course Niemeyer would give him irrefutable arguments to support it, whereas if he refused to adopt it he would be faced with criticisms from the City authorities against which he would not have any effective answer.'[259] Second, the rise in the dollar exchange after the election of the Conservative Government, combined with the determination of the Bank and permanent Treasury officials to attempt to hold on to any appreciation if possible, meant that, as most of Churchill's advisers pointed out, the additional adjustments necessary to achieve parity were relatively small, perhaps even smaller than those necessary to hold the exchange given the expectations and elements of speculation that existed at the time. Given these propensities a decision not to go back in 1925 could have been made and announced in the summer or autumn of 1924, but not after the Conservatives' electoral success and the subsequent revision of expectations. Third, the evidence presented to the Chancellor probably eased the decision, for it emphasised the benefits of restoration, largely in terms of employment and trade, and minimised the problems both of adjustment to the new parity and of management at the new parity after the period of adjustment. This minimisation depended, to a considerable extent, in the first instance, on an expectation of inflationary developments abroad. It also depended on a concentration on the dollar exchange and a complete refusal to consider possible paths of development on the Continent, particularly the exchange rates chosen in the process of possible future stabilisations and the recovery of Germany from her post-war problems. After 1925, the low rates of stabilisation chosen by France and Belgium were often referred to as sources of difficulty, despite the fact that the possibilities of stabilising at such rates which reflected exchange conditions more than price conditions, had been foreseen as early as 1922.[260] True, Churchill was aware of Keynes' arguments against restoration in the spring of 1925, but his was very much a voice in the wilderness, and a very ambiguous one at that given his inflationary expectations and his frequent failure to distinguish clearly between the short and the long run. Finally, much of the public antagonism to such a decision had disappeared, partially because the unique connection between the gold standard and deflation had apparently ceased to hold with the managed money school's acceptance of the March 1925 increase in Bank Rate, that symbol of deflation, and with the rise in the exchange after October 1924 which had occurred without outward and visible signs of deflation.[261] Even the Federation of British Industry, one of Keynes' chief sources of support on previous occasions, accepted that other considerations might make restoration necessary and that on a longer view such a decision 'would be greatly to the benefit of British Industry' even though it might necessitate some short-term deflation.[262] To these considerations, Churchill certainly added an element of faith in the policy's success as his disillusioned reaction to the results and his subsequent bitterness towards the Governor indicate.[263]

More generally, the decision to return to the gold standard at pre-war par was more or less inevitable, particularly after the rise in the dollar exchange. Successive governments had committed themselves to such a policy goal; the overwhelming majority of opinion accepted it; the specialists in the Bank, the Treasury and the Chamberlain—Bradbury Committee were prepared to force the necessary adjustments. Economic analysis, as such, had little to do with the decision: analysts such as Pigou merely played a 'priestly' role, justifying decisions taken for more deep-seated reasons.[264] Pigou, with characteristic honesty, admitted as much in his evidence before the Macmillan Committee:[265]

> 'Prior to that it had been the decided policy of all Governments to go back to gold and, as a matter of practice, it was felt that nothing else could be done. No politician at the time advocated not going back to the gold system ... . The real practical alternative in my view was to go back now or later. It may have been wrong. Of course one might be apt to say that it was wrong because gold is not so sacred as it was, but this was very soon after an inflation, and my impression of the general atmosphere was that it was quite impossible then to have done anything else ... . If you did narrow the issue to that the argument for returning now was this: You have to take the plunge, the water is not terribly cold now; it is a gamble whether it will be colder later on. Get it over ... . I thought the politician would make the plunge anyway.'

The deep-seated reasons which provided the motivation to take the plunge had their roots in banking and financial attitudes towards gold, debt repayment and good faith which were essentially moral, and in a deep faith in the mechanisms of the pre-war gold standard.[266]

III   The Implications of $4.86 chap 2

Before one can assess the consequences of the return to gold at $4.86, one must first have a set of criteria for the evaluation of exchange rate choices. In purely theoretical terms, the notion of the unique, policy-free equilibrium rate of exchange which implies equilibrium in the balance of payments is, as Professor Joan Robinson has indicated, a chimera.[1] For given market supply and demand conditions there are an infinite number of 'equilibrium' rates which correspond to varying mixes of monetary, trade, fiscal and other policies.[2] Thus a much more fruitful approach to the problem of exchange rate choice in 1925, would be one which took account of the international and domestic policy goals of the Authorities and looked at the choice of $4.86 as one which would or would not allow their successful realisation.

The Goals of Policy

As the Authorities, either in or after 1925, never really adopted this approach and never set out their policy goals in relation to the exchange rate under discussion, one is forced to search for what appear to have been their implicit goals. In this light, the evidence suggests, that an appropriate exchange rate would have allowed 'full employment' at, say, the pre-war average of 95.3 per cent of the labour force;[3] a surplus on income account sufficient to allow unrestricted foreign lending; and the maintenance of free trade with the minimal pre-1931 exceptions.* The implicit pre-war employment standard existed in some of the pre-gold standard discussions and in the frequent post-1925 Treasury pressure for moderation in the Bank's policies.[4] It also found use in much of the political debate of the period and in many of Keynes' discussions of post-1925 policy.[5] The ideal of unrestricted foreign lending hung heavily over much of the discussion that led up to the return to gold and it lay at the roots of the official hostility after 1925 to such controls on overseas lending as proved expedient. In this respect, the *Report* of the Overseas Loans Subcommittee of the Committee of Civil Research is instructive.[6] The goal of free trade never became completely

---

* To these one might add a desire for a stabilised (and by implication stable) international economic system which would have allowed the growth of trade and investment. As this would have probably come with any stable rate, at least to some extent, the analysis below excludes this matter. It also excludes any specification of the trade-offs between goals.

explicit in public other than in practice. However, during the Macmillan Committee's drafting discussions when the alternatives of devaluation and protection were discussed with specific reference to exchange policy, a standard of judgement in the minds of two of those involved in the 1925 decision became clear:[7]

'Lord Bradbury: I am afraid of tampering with Free Trade, and I am also afraid of tampering with the gold standard. If I had to choose between tampering with the gold standard as a remedy and Protection, I should be solid for tampering with the gold standard. I should much prefer it to Protection.

'Mr. Bevin: I agree.

'Mr. Lubbock: I should be very sorry to think that the choice of one of these was the dilemma.

'Lord Bradbury: So should I.'

When to these specific goals one adds the desire to keep London as an international financial centre of the first rank, something that repeatedly appeared in policy discussions of the period,[8] it becomes clear that the overall goal of the Authorities might be summed up as one to maintain, as far as possible, the pre-1914 position. Whether the return to gold at the pre-war par was consistent with this overall goal is the basic question.

Any attempt to evaluate the 1925 decision on this basis must compare the overall goal with the international position of the British economy in 1924–25 as compared to that of a typical pre-war year. Such a comparison must take into account not only the basic trade, invisibles and capital positions but also the availability and effectiveness of the policy instruments available to the Authorities. Thus the earlier discussion of the international position of the British economy in 1924 becomes extremely relevant.[9] That discussion indicated that, despite the virtual elimination of Germany as a major competitor, British trade performance in 1924 as compared to 1913 was probably worse than world performance, although marginally better than overall European performance including that of Germany. It also indicated that British imports, despite the depreciated exchange, had grown faster than world imports; that the British invisibles position was weaker than pre-war and that the evolution in the pattern of settlements probably placed greater demands on the U.K. At the same time as these underlying changes occurred, the movement towards a decentralised international financial system increased the possibilities of strain on the exchange position and of policy conflicts, while the evolution of financial instruments and institutions made the traditional instruments of policy less effective. Given these underlying changes, the basic criterion for an evaluation of the exchange rate chosen in 1925 could be summed up as follows: as the international position of Great Britain was, in many respects, weaker than that before 1914, any exchange rate policy which did not improve her trading, competitive and policy-making position vis-a-vis that of a typical pre-war year was unwise. Given this criterion, the long-standing debate as to whether sterling was overvalued in 1925 takes on its relevance.

Was Sterling Overvalued at $4.86?

Most observers since Keynes have accepted that in 1925 sterling was overvalued by at least 10 per cent at the pre-1914 parity of $4.86.[10] However, there has been a significant undercurrent of opinion that has rejected or seriously questioned Keynes' overvaluation argument, its most important contributors being Professors Youngson, Morgan and Gregory.[11] In many senses, the argument as to whether sterling was overvalued or not on a purchasing-power parity basis is rather irrelevant to the point at issue, for it would seem that given the changes in the international position of the United Kingdom since 1913 any exchange rate that did not somewhat undervalue sterling on such a basis would, given the goals of the Authorities, probably have been unfortunate. However, given the heat generated by the debate, both at the time and occasionally since, a re-examination of the statistics and the issues is worthwhile.

The standard method used for testing an exchange rate for overvaluation involves the use of purchasing-power parity calculations, which as noted above played a relatively minor direct role in the actual decision.* Stated in its comparative form, the theory of purchasing-power parity 'asserts that the equilibrium exchange rate moves parallel with the ratio of the movements in the two countries of the price levels over time.'[12] If, so the argument runs, comparing two countries from a base year in which the exchange rate was in 'equilibrium', the price level has doubled in country A and trebled in country B, then the 'equilibrium' exchange rate (units of A's currency per unit of B's) will have changed in the ratio of 2/3. So stated, the theory appears to be extremely simple to use as a guide to the appropriate exchange rate between two currencies, but this simplicity hides two basic problems: which are the relevant price levels for comparisons and which additional assumptions underlying the statements are relevant to the particular case at hand.

The choice of the appropriate price level for comparisons boils down to a decision as to which is the most appropriate price index for international comparisons of competitiveness. The traditional choice has been an index of wholesale prices and this index found considerable use during the period under consideration, largely as a result of its ready availability.[13] However, such an index, particularly in an open economy, consists largely of price observations for the staple commodities of international trade. For these commodities, and for an index heavily weighted with such goods, prices in domestic currency will reflect changes in foreign exchange rates reasonably accurately. Thus any comparison based on such prices would tell one very little about the implications of exchange rate choices or existing exchange levels as it would contain very few quotations that reflected domestic costs.[14] Thus one begins a search for alternatives. An index of export prices seems, at first glance, to be a useful

---

* This is not to deny that the habits of thought engendered by the discussion of such calculations did not thoroughly permeate the atmosphere in which the discussions occurred.

possibility and as such it has found use in one discussion of the 1925 decision.[15] However, export prices may also prove poor indicators of the implications of exchange rate choices, for although they do contain elements of domestic costs they relate only to goods exported. If goods are in perfect competition internationally, differences in relative prices between countries will not be reflected in indices of export prices but rather in market shares. Even where goods are in imperfect competition internationally, in the short period firms may continue to export at the world price and absorb increased production costs by reducing profit margins. Firms may also reduce their selling effort while continuing to accept orders at the world price, and thus reduced competitiveness would again appear as a loss in market share rather than an increase in relative price.[16] The imperfections of export prices as indices of international competitive conditions are apparent in the recent devaluation of sterling when British firms raised their exports prices in sterling by more than the cost increases implicit in the devaluation and the associated increases in taxation would warrant in order to reconstitute profit margins that had been previously squeezed by high relative British costs; whereas, foreign exporters raised their sterling selling prices by less than the depreciation of sterling by reducing profit margins to maintain markets. Other attempts to choose an appropriate price index have involved the use of more domestically oriented indices of relative costs, particularly the one implicit in the cost of living or retail price index.[17] However, as this is a highly sectional index, usually heavily weighted towards the consumption patterns of working people, it may be inappropriate as a guide to the costs faced by producers of export or import-competing goods and services. However, it has the advantages of being relatively immune to divergent structural changes over time and of being representative of a large class of expenditures. Another possible index is the national income implicit price deflator. Such an index, although subject to divergent structural changes over time when two countries are compared, is a composite index reflecting changes in the prices of various goods and services in the economy. In use such deflators for two countries have proved to be 'fairly good rivals of consumer prices' in purchasing-power parity calculations.[18] However, even here, service prices provide a source of difficulty, for these are not equalised by trade and tend to reflect international differences in wages and manufacturing productivity.[19] Thus the evidence would indicate that for purchasing-power parity calculations, most indices contain problems, but that in many repects consumer prices and national income deflators might provide useful indices of relative domestic costs for exchange rate calculations.

However, even if the indices chosen are relatively appropriate, a second problem still faces the analyst, the problem of structural changes. Over the period of years normally chosen for purchasing-power parity calculations other things do not remain equal or change in the two countries concerned in offsetting directions. Changes in tastes, technology, tariffs, international investment and trading positions, and internal relationships in the economies concerned can occur and undermine any direct comparisons of costs, prices, competitiveness and balance in a nation's international accounts, particularly, when such balance depends on much more than the trading position for which purchasing-power parity calculations are most relevant.[20] However, such indices, if used cautiously, can be 'of considerable diagnostic value' in discussions of exchange rate choice.[21] Nevertheless, after major international changes such as those involved in a world war and its aftermath such calculations require considerable additional evidence to support their use; and one must never forget that the appropriate exchange rate in relation to any one currency depends on the exchange rates prevailing (or likely to prevail) in third countries as well.

Putting this last point to one side for the moment, despite its implications, Table 3 presents a variety of estimates of purchasing-power parities for the sterling—dollar exchange between 1923 and 1927. The estimates used are all annual averages, as quotations for individual months are not available for some series and are subject to random influences such as bad harvests for others. The estimates include those most commonly used in the debates of the period and since, as well as others added at this time. The indices of unemployment and unit wage costs in manufacturing appear at the bottom as indicators of more general economic conditions.

The figures presented in Table 3, although conflicting, are illuminating. Using indices of wholesale prices, those most frequently employed in 1925, sterling was not overvalued at the time of the return to gold. However, the same indices indicate that sterling was slightly undervalued in 1927, a situation that seems difficult to believe and which no one has subsequently suggested. The export price indices indicate that sterling was significantly undervalued in 1923 and 1924 and slightly undervalued in 1925. Unfortunately the Federal Reserve Board ceased publication of the export price indices at the end of 1925 so that later comparisons are impossible. The retail price indices conflict. The Massachusetts' index, the index of retail prices for the United States regularly quoted by the *Federal Reserve Bulletin* and used by Keynes in his discussions of the return to gold, when used with the U.K. Ministry of Labour cost of living index suggests that sterling was significantly overvalued in 1925 and thereafter and slightly overvalued in 1924. The fact that this index only applied to one state led Professor Gregory to challenge Keynes' use of the Massachusetts' index and to use the more general Bureau of Labor index to argue that the difficulties of the British position stemmed from the transition from an undervalued exchange to parity.[22] Significantly, however, Professor Gregory did not proceed to argue that sterling was slightly undervalued thereafter on the basis of the same index, despite several opportunities to do so. The League of Nations' index of American retail prices which does not seem to have found use in 1925, or thereafter, follows the Massachusetts' index in indicating that sterling was overvalued in 1925, although by a lesser amount than the use of the latter index would indicate. The more general implicit G.N.P. deflators indicate that sterling was overvalued throughout the period covered by the series in Table 3. This overvaluation occurred, despite the effect on the service component of the U.S. index of the faster rise in American money wages during the period after 1913.

Table 3. Selected indices of purchasing-power parity for the sterling–dollar exchange, 1923–27.

(U.S. price index as a percentage of U.K.)

Basis of Comparison	1923	1924	1925	1927
Sterling Exchange as a percentage of par	94.0	90.8	99.2	99.9
Wholesale Prices – 1913 = 100 U.S. & U.K. – Federal Reserve	96.8	90.1	100	n.a.
Wholesale Prices – 1913 = 100 U.S. – Bureau of Labor U.K. – Board of Trade	97.0	90.3	99.1	103.4
Export Prices – 1913 = 100 U.S. & U.K. – Federal Reserve	103.4	98.8	104.1	n.a.
Retail Prices – 1914 = 100 U.S. – Bureau of Labor U.K. – Ministry of Labour	97.5	97.3	99.2	103.1
Retail Prices – 1914 = 100 U.S. – Massachusetts U.K. – Ministry of Labour	89.8	89.2	91.1	93.2
Retail Prices – July 1914 = 100 U.S. – League of Nations U.K. – Ministry of Labour	93.6	93.7	95.5	97.6
Implicit G.N.P. Deflator 1907–1911 = 100 U.S. – Kuznets U.K. – Peacock and Wiseman	n.a.	88	89	90
Reference Indices Unemployment – 1912–14 = 100				
U.S. – L.C.E.S.	42.9	89.3	57.1	58.9
U.K. – Trade Union	393.7	282.2	365.8	n.a.
– Unemployment Insurance	407.6	358.9	393.7	337.9
Unit Wage Costs – 1913 = 100				
U.S.	176.6	173.4	164.1	157.5
U.K.	n.a.	168.0	167.2	162.2

n.a. – not available.

Sources: 1. E.H. Phelps Brown and M.H. Browne, *A Century of Pay*, (London, 1968), Appendix III and Table 19.

2. Federal Reserve Board, *Federal Reserve Bulletin*.

3. League of Nations, *International Statistical Yearbook, 1929*, (Geneva, 1930), Table 109.

Notes to Table 3 *continued:-*

Sources: 4. London and Cambridge Economic Service, *The British Economy, Key Statistics, 1900–1966*, (London, n.d.), Tables E and O.

5. B.R. Mitchell and P. Deane, *Abstract of British Historical Statistics*, (Cambridge, 1962), Labour Force 3.

6. A.T. Peacock and J.Wiseman, *The Growth of Public Expenditure in the United Kingdom*, (London, 1961), Table A3.

7. U.S. Department of Commerce, *Historical Statistics of the United States from Colonial Times to 1957*, (Washington, 1960), Series E 113, F 1–5.

On balance, these estimates must be regarded as conflicting. However, given the differing behaviour of the series for unemployment and unit wage costs in the two countries, the deterioration in Britain's international financial position and the transformation of America's international position, including the tariff increases of 1921, one would incline towards the position that an exchange rate which did not undervalue sterling vis-a-vis the dollar was probably too high. As even the most optimistic indices for purchasing power parity calculations hardly did that, and as the most pessimistic indices suggested an overvaluation of as much as ten per cent, one would incline towards the view that given official policy goals sterling was significantly overvalued at the exchange rate chosen in 1925. An exchange rate perhaps 10 per cent lower than $4.86 would probably have been somewhat more appropriate for sterling.

The overvaluation of sterling implicit in the purchasing-power parity and related indices for the sterling–dollar exchange becomes more striking if the position of sterling vis-a-vis other European currencies enters into consideration. Niemeyer's expectation that the stabilisation of sterling might encourage other European stabilisations was, to some extent, reasonable, but his implicit expectation that they would do so in a manner which would not affect the viability of certain exchange rates chosen for sterling was not.[23] The German stabilisation of 1923–24 with its undervaluation of the mark suggested a route that other European countries might conceivably choose to follow in their stabilisation policies.* Given the possibility of undervaluations occurring elsewhere and given the existing uncertainty as to European rates of stabilisation, there was a strong case for waiting somewhat longer before fixing a par value for sterling. The unsettled conditions in France and Belgium could not continue for ever, no matter what the British decided to do, and a year's wait might have clarified and

---

* Using unit wage costs as a rough index of competitiveness, taking 1913 = 100, German costs in 1925 were 147.7 as compared with 167.2 for the U.K. and 164.1 for the U.S. at a time when the three countries' exchange rates bore the same par value relationship to each other as in 1913. (Brown and Browne, *op. cit.*, Appendix III and Table 19.) The possibility of undervaluation had certainly been discussed in reference to exchange choices before 1925. (Gregory, *op. cit.*, Ch. 1.)

stabilised the situation sufficiently to allow a co-ordinated return to gold at mutually convenient exchange rates. However, throughout the discussions surrounding the return to gold, no one really considered the implications or probabilities of European exchange rate choices affecting sterling, although after the event these same rate choices found use as one explanation of the problems that beset the British economy after 1925.[24] Those entrusted with advising the Chancellor on the return to gold did not even pay attention to the implications of the German stabilisation that antedated the giving of that advice or to the effects of the certain revival of German competition on sterling's prospects. The concentration on the dollar as the only gold currency excluded that, as did the tendency to regard 1925 as a return to gold rather than as the choice of an exchange rate which carried multilateral implications. The results of this dollar-centred, gold-centred view were, to say the least, unfortunate.

The Balance of Payments and $4.86

The overvaluation of sterling had implications for the balance of trade and the balance on invisibles which weakened sterling's international position still further. It would tend to reduce exports and raise imports of goods by amounts dependent on the relevant cost conditions, supply and demand elasticities, and businiessmen's reactions. Although the statistical difficulties are legion,[25] the evidence from the numerous attempts to measure the various relevant elasticities suggests that the price mechanism remains relatively powerful in international trade and that any overvaluation of sterling would lead to a significant deterioration on trade account.[26]* On the income from invisibles, an over-valuation of sterling would also have important effects.† Income from shipping would tend to deteriorate as British prices and/or costs would be above those of competitors who could increase their share of the market through straight price competition or greater selling effort. The income from fixed interest investments would remain largely unchanged as most British foreign investment was denominated in sterling, although the costs of servicing British debt would rise for foreigners in terms of their own currencies. This might increase the incidence of bad debts and thus reduce sterling investment income somewhat, but this would be unlikely in a period of international prosperity. Income from overseas equities would be reduced, as dividends were determined by profits in foreign countries. On Government account, overvaluation would reduce the sterling costs of servicing war debts, but leave the value of war debt payments to the U.K. unchanged as these were denominated in sterling. Overvaluation would, however, reduce the sterling value of reparation receipts which were denominated in gold. It would also tend to reduce the income from banking and

---

* See the Appendix for some rough calculations of the effects of the appreciation of sterling.

† All subsequent references are to incomes in sterling unless explicitly noted.

insurance commissions and the like, for incomes here are largely the result of percentage commissions. For the foreigner, exchange overvaluation would mean that he would need less insurance in sterling to cover a foreign risk of a given size or a smaller sterling bill to finance a trade transaction of a given size. Therefore, with a given volume of business, sterling proceeds would fall. Of course a stable exchange might increase such business, but this increase in business and the resulting increase in incomes would result from stability or from a growth in the volume of foreign risks requiring insurance or trade requiring finance and not from an overvaluation of the sterling exchange. The income from miscellaneous invisibles would probably also fall as a result of overvaluation. Recent research[27] has indicated that tourism earnings are very sensitive to changes in exchange rates, although the effects in the 1920s when the average tourist may have been less price conscious and determined to visit the mother country may not have been as great. Emigrants' remittances would probably also fall in terms of sterling in that they largely originated outside the U.K. and depended on external conditions for their determination. The overvaluation of sterling would also reduce sterling receipts for used ships to some extent, but it would leave royalty payments from the U.K. unchanged to a great extent, although it might reduce the sterling value of royalty incomes. Thus the effects of sterling's overvaluation on the balance of current account would be mixed. There is little indication that the improvement in the Government's debt servicing position would offset the losses on trade, shipping, short-interest and commissions, miscellaneous invisibles and probably non-sterling denominated foreign investment or equity incomes. Thus from a balance of payments point of view, in the short-term, overvaluation would hardly make sense.

The additional deterioration in the international position of Great Britain implicit in the overvaluation of sterling that the above considerations suggest would have repercussions on the domestic economy. The rise in imports and the decline in exports would, assuming the Authorities did nothing to offset them, have multiplier effects, which, although they would improve the balance of payments position to some extent, would reduce domestic incomes and employment. These effects would tend to be cumulative to some extent, for an uncompetitive economy would share less in the overall growth of the world economy and would be hurt more by a fall in world incomes, as it would tend to become the high cost marginal supplier in many instances — last engaged and first dismissed. In so far as the induced effects of these changes affected the domestic climate of enterprise the overvaluation would have more serious effects in that it would affect future investment and hence future growth prospects. Any reduction in investment would have further effects on competitiveness, for it is largely through investment that innovations take effect.[28] These effects on future prospects postulated thus far are independent of those which would follow an effort by the Authorities to improve the balance of payments by domestic deflation.

As previous discussions have indicated, those advising the Chancellor to return to gold had generally admitted that this act of policy would leave sterling somewhat overvalued and that some adjustment in relative costs would be necessary, if only to prevent deterioration in the balance of payments. They were unsure as to the amount of adjustment required, but as they generally judged the necessary amount through a comparison of British and American wholesale price indices they were naturally convinced that it was relatively slight. As to the means of adjustment, their attitudes were vague and conflicting, but, aside from some expansion of exports, domestic activity and employment which they believed would accompany the resulting European stability and recovery, they recognised that either their competitors' prices and costs would have to rise or British prices and costs would have to fall. Some combination of these two routes was also possible. Generally speaking, none of Churchill's advisers contemplated the possibility of having to reduce British prices and costs more quickly than those of her competitors.[29]

As to possible means of adjustment if British prices and costs proved to be those which required absolute reduction as relief from foreign sources proved insufficient or unavailable, the Chancellor's advisers admitted that some deflation operating along the lines outlined by the Cunliffe and subsequent official committees would be necessary.[30]* Through a high Bank Rate and restrictive credit policies domestic activity would be depressed by an amount sufficient to produce a volume of unemployment large enough to allow reductions in money wages to be successfully carried through by employers. If the necessary adjustment involved was only 1—2 per cent, such a policy on the basis of pre-war experience could be regarded as possible, although unfortunate, for the pre-war period had seen several occasions when money wages fell by that amount in the course of a year or so.[31] However, if the necessary adjustment involved was in the range of 5—10 per cent or more, then pre-war experience provided no examples. The only available example of large reductions in wages came from the period of the post-war slump of 1920—22. Between their peak in January 1921 and their nadir in December 1922 average weekly wage rates fell by 38 per cent; while the cost of living fell by over 50 per cent.[32] However, a large proportion of these reductions were accomplished under sliding scale agreements through which wages were related to the cost of living.[33] After the experiences of 1921—22 such agreements naturally became much less popular and this change meant that this 'easy' route could be less relied on in future, even if the cause of the fall in the cost of living was an international slump.[34] Future reductions would depend more on great industrial disputes such as those in coal and engineering during 1921—22 and on unemployment levels. However, in future even reductions of this sort might become more difficult to achieve, for real wages in the unsheltered trades,

---

* Other possible means were not discussed. The Appendix gives some indication as to a few of the additional possibilities available.

those which would be first affected by the overvaluation of sterling, had fallen in the post-1920 slump to levels below those of 1914 and workers in these trades would be extremely resistant to the further reductions in money and real wages which the successful restoration of gold at an overvalued exchange required. Thus the task which the Authorities set themselves in 1925 was potentially extremely difficult. If American prices failed to rise as expected by an amount sufficient to remove a large part of the overvaluation of sterling or if third countries stabilised at relatively low exchange rates, the burden for official financial policy would be particularly great. If the calculations of the Authorities as to the overvaluation of sterling were inaccurate in a conservative direction, as previous discussions have suggested, the necessary reductions in British wages were of an order of magnitude which would be extremely difficult to achieve without great industrial disputes, social strife and unemployment. If the prices of Britain's competitors fell, of course the reductions would have to be greater, provided that the increase in British productivity was not above that of her competitors, which it was not.[35] However, any difficulties that arose after 1925 in this respect would be less the result of any fall in foreign prices and costs than of the basic decisions of 1925, for these implied that the economy would be subject to considerable stress largely as a result of national economic policy.

The discussion of the previous paragraphs suggests that the overvaluation of sterling in 1925 impaired Britain's international position, already weakened by the War and its aftermath, and left British society open to the possibilities of great internal strains resulting from efforts to make a go of attempts to successfully adjust to $4.86. It suggests as well that some deliberate undervaluation of sterling to offset the unfavourable longer term structural effects of the War would have been advisable. This would have been true even if other European countries had not, sensibly and thoughtfully in many respects,[36] undervalued their currencies when they devalued and returned to gold. The addition of overvaluation plus undervaluation elsewhere to a difficult underlying internal economic position laid the basis for many of the peculiarly British problems of the later 1920s. A lower rate of exchange in 1925, although it would certainly not have solved all the problems of the British economy in the 1920s, as it will not solve all the problems of the later 1960s, cetainly would have provided a better basis on which to solve those problems which centred around the transition of the industrial structure from the nineteenth to the twentieth century. A lower parity might, as Clay suggests,[37] have had to have been supported at some time by credit restriction, and industry and finance might have been forced to adjust to external conditions. Such a possibility exists under any system of fixed exchange rates. However, it was one thing to ask the British economy of 1925 to face an initial adjustment resulting from overvaluation and to run the risk of additional adjustments resulting from changes in international conditions, and another to ask the same economy only to accept the risk of the latter, particularly when a more buoyant British economy, the world's largest importer and traditional lender, would have had favourable repercussion effects elsewhere.

However, such more general considerations did not enter the minds of most observers in 1924—25. Gold at any rate other than $4.86 was unthinkable. The tendency to simplify the decision to one of gold at a given rate or of no gold at all rather than to consider the possibility of gold at alternative rates of exchange represents one of the most tragic aspects of the decision-making process. It meant that once gold as a system became official policy the British economy had to adjust, or not adjust, as best it could to the new circumstances, for throughout policy thinking ruled out the possibility of gold plus deliberate external adjustment. The resulting attempts at adjustment form a central theme for much of the economic history of the period after 1925.

V Conclusion

The 'Norman Conquest of 4.86'[1] was ultimately an act of faith in an incompletely understood adjustment mechanism undertaken largely for moral reasons. It implied a belief that any overvaluation that did exist would be removed by reductions in British, or rises in American, prices and costs, that the results would be 'good for trade' in the sense that Britain's example would induce stabilisations elsewhere and that a stable international environment would provide a basis for expanding trade which would benefit an internationally oriented economy such as Britain's. Looking back on the event five years later Lord Bradbury and Cecil Lubbock, the Deputy Governor of the Bank up to March 1925, admitted as much:[2]

'Lord Bradbury: ... There was no doubt at all when we returned to the Gold Standard we rather hoped that adjustment would take place through a rise in other people's prices and not a fall in ours.

'Mr. Lubbock: Other people's had been rising.

'Lord Bradbury: In spite of that, we got a world fall, not a very heavy one which superimposed on our own, made our task more difficult.

. . .

'I suppose it was altruism largely ... . To some extent altruism and to some extent a general feeling that unless and until other people returned to gold our trade must suffer. There was at that time, a very great feeling that our export trade was being cut into by the low prices in foreign markets which could be accepted by countries with depreciated currencies.

'Mr. Lubbock: The idea was to get the world on a common denominator for their money so that international trade and international investment might result ... . It may be ... we thought more of getting the world on a common denominator and making it possible to have international trade on an international basis than what the price level ought to be.'

Once that decision was made, and announced, there was no going back on it. The exchange rate for sterling, given the changes in Britain's international position since 1913 and the policy goals of the Authorities, definitely overvalued sterling, probably by at least 10 per cent. The years after 1925 saw the trend in international prices moving downwards, not upwards as Churchill's advisers (as well as Keynes and McKenna) had expected. American wholesale prices reached their 1925–31 peak early in 1925 and then fell until late 1927, rose slightly in 1928 and wobbled slightly until September 1929 before falling without interruption until the end of the inter-war gold standard period. This declining trend made the task of relative cost reduction much more difficult, for it almost ensured that British money wages would have to fall absolutely if the policy adopted in 1925 was to bear its full fruit. After a brief rise in 1925, British money wages did fall back slightly, while money wages abroad continued to rise until 1929.[3] However, when these divergent wage trends are combined with trend in productivity the evolution of the British competitive position is clear. Table 4 presents indices of unit wage costs in industry. Given that in 1925 the mark had been undervalued and sterling overvalued, and that the rise in German unit wage costs did not completely erode this advantage vis-a-vis the U.K. until 1929, the competitive pressures operative on Britain after 1925 are immediately apparent. If the undervaluation of the French franc, in terms of unit wage costs, throughout the period is added to the figures presented below,[4] the severity of the adjustment problem and its exacerbation after 1925 are even more striking.

Table 4.   Unit Wage Costs in Industry in Four Countries, 1925—31 (1925 = 100)

Country	1925	1926	1927	1928	1929	1930	193
U.K.	100	100	97	97	95	92	9(
Germany	100	102	101	106	112	113	10{
U.S.	100	98	96	93	90	88	7{
Sweden	100	90	87	88	80	72	7(

Source: E.H. Phelps Brown and M.H. Browne, *A Century of Pay*, (London, 1968) Appendix III.

Further evidence as to the extent of the competitive disadvantage of British exports after 1925 and its implications has been provided by Maizels' study which uses 1913 and 1929 as benchmark years.[5] Between these two dates, Britain's share of world trade in manufactures fell from 30.2 per cent to 23.0 per cent (22.4 per cent if figures for the Netherlands are included for 1929).[6] This decline in share occurred in all major commodity groups and in most individual markets.[7] Between 1913 and 1929, U.K. exports of manufactures fell by $140 million at 1913 prices; whereas, world market growth and the area and commodity pattern of Britain's 1913 trade would have led one to expect an increase of $730 million at 1913 prices.[8] The implication is that losses in market share rather than the area or commodity pattern of British trade accounted for Britain's export problems in the world economy of the period. Much of the explanation for this poor market performance would appear to lie in the realm of price competitiveness, for comparing 1929 with 1913 the unit values of the U.K.'s manufactured exports rose by 13 per cent more than those of her competitors.[9] Although some of this deterioration might reflect quality changes in British exports, it is unlikely that the improvement in Britain's relative position in this area was so marked as to remove the suspicion that she became less competitive during the period. The suspicion is reinforced by the heavy losses suffered by

British manufactured exports from import substitution in both industrial and semi-industrial markets. Given Britain's heavy concentration of 40 per cent of her manufactured exports in semi-industrial markets in 1913, as compared to her competitors' 10–15 per cent, she was more prone to such losses, but her high prices and costs also left her in a more exposed position.[10] Such losses had extensive repercussion effects on the U.K., for even in the relatively unprosperous late 1920's exports accounted for 37 per cent of manufacturing output (45 per cent in 1913) and demand declines in this area could have powerful effects on industrial profits, investment and innovation which could be cumulative.[11] The major concern at this point, however, remains the fall in British export competitiveness, some of which may have resulted from changing demand patterns within Maizels' broader classes and changing institutional relationships, but much of which apparently resulted from a deterioration in price competitiveness and its surrounding determinants — range, quality, delivery dates, marketing, etc. — and would partially qualify as a result of the decisions of 1925.

In these circumstances, the tasks of internal adjustment were substantial, but after the General Strike of 1926 direct attacks on money wages were not really possible. Thus the success of the 1925 policy became dependent on British money wages remaining constant while competitors' money wages rose by amounts sufficient to more than offset their higher rates of growth of productivity. In a world of steady or slightly falling prices, this meant that the process of adjustment, rather than being relatively easy as Churchill's advisers were wont to suggest and as some outside observers believed,[12] would be a long drawn out process, easily threatened by developments elsewhere and inhibited by policy preferences at home.

In the interim, the Authorities had to make the best of a situation in which there were three parameters: the exchange rate, the level of money wages, and a general unwillingness to take any fundamental steps to improve the situation.[13] The overvaluation of sterling after 1925 and subsequent decisions taken in countries such as France meant that the exchanges were perpetually weak, despite the historically high rates of unemployment. For example, the median exchange rates for all the principal exchanges after 1925 were well below the par of exchange; whereas, before 1914 they had tended to be near but slightly below par in the case of Paris and above par in the cases of Berlin and New York.[14] This weakness existed despite an alteration of both short- and long-term interest differentials in London's favour between the pre-war and post-war periods.[15] The exchange weakness reflected itself in the tendency of the free market price of gold in London to remain at or near the Bank of England's selling price, except for brief intervals, throughout the entire post-war gold standard period.[16] Although both the Bank and the Treasury pursued mildly deflationary policies before 1929 and somewhat more intensely deflationary policies thereafter, domestic political pressures prevented any attempts to find a solution through intense deflation. In the meantime, with the exchanges under pressure, and further deflation along orthodox Cunliffe Committee lines largely ruled out,[17] the Bank of England, and to a lesser extent the Treasury, faced a situation that offered almost certain prospects of reserve losses with little probability of reserve gains. Given the constraints that existed on aggregate policies, the Authorities began, simultaneously with the return to gold, to develop policies which would substitute for Bank Rate policy in varying degrees in controlling the international payments of the British economy and even allow reserve gains on occasion. The approach basically consisted of the adoption of short-term palliatives which would hold the position but which would contribute little towards the solution of longer term adjustment problems.[18] The policies adopted — active foreign exchange and gold market operations, 'controls' on overseas lending both long and short-term, and devices to change the relationship between domestic and international interest rates — all served to insulate the domestic economy, to some extent, from international pressures and to allow considerable non-adjustment to coexist with a reasonable level of international reserves. Many of these policies represented innovations in Bank of England policy and represent early uses of policy instruments refined in the period after 1931, but they did not substantially alter the underlying situation of sterling's overvaluation: they, plus the attraction of substantial short-term foreign balances to London, merely masked it. With their emphasis on correction or concealment rather than adjustment they undermined, in many repects, the liberal international economy the return to the gold standard was supposed to symbolise.[19] As Keynes put it in a rewiew of Bradbury's 'The Coal Crisis and the Gold Standard', expedients were used to defend the parity 'which in the old days would have shocked Lord Bradbury out of his skin'.[20] As the Overseas Loans Sub-Committee's *Report* and his Macmillan Committee Memorandum of Dissent indicate, Bradbury was duly shocked and most 'orthodox' in his response, as were others.[21]

However, this is running ahead of events, as the basic concern is with the decision to return to gold. That decision, as noted above was ultimately much more the result of beliefs than of analysis. To a certain extent, the Chancellor was misled by his civil servants and the Governor. In the discussions prior to March 20, with the exception of the famous McKenna, Keynes, Bradbury, Niemeyer dinner party of 17 March, the problem of adjustment was never squarely faced, until after the event, except in euphemisms such as 'sacrifice'. There appears to have been an assumption that if deflation was necessary, wages would show their post-1920 flexibility, but this was implied and assumed rather than analysed. Except for some rudimentary calculations of purchasing-power parity, which were only partially believed — and therefore never fully analysed for their implications — and which used only wholesale prices, there was basically no consideration of the adjustments necessary to make $4.86 a success. The trade position and the effects of exchange appreciation thereon were never really considered, except in the most general terms, and the time path of adjustment was ignored. As for the capital account, observers assumed that there would be few problems in the return to gold and that alterations in Bank Rate could cope with anything that subsequently arose.

n fact, much of the case for a return to gold, as presented by Churchill's advisers, depended upon a widespread expectation of inflation. This expectation was certainly very general: it extended to Keynes who had used the high probability of American inflation as one of the arguments for a managed currency;[22] had welcomed the Gold Standard Act on a misreading which led him to believe that the Act removed the Banks' obligation to buy gold at a fixed price and thus, in theory at least, allowed the bank to insulate Britain from inflationary movements abroad through exchange appreciation;[23] and had found in an expectation of American inflation his ray of hope for an easy adjustment after the event.[24] Such an expectation depended on 'a nice balance ... between skill and want of skill on the part of the Federal Reserve Board', for it required 'that the Federal Reserve Board should lose control of their own situation and should then begin to exercise skill just at the time that our own policy requires that they should'.[25] If it didn't assume this, it was a ploy to 'give businessmen the tonic of a little inflation under highly respectable auspices'.[26] This expectation certainly weakened Keynes' case against returning in many eyes and it also precluded much serious analysis of the adjustment problem,[27] as did one additional assumption.

This second important assumption underlying the 1925 discussions was that the Bank would, as a minimum, attempt to maintain any improvements in the exchange. If, in addition to this, one assumed that there was a substantial volume of speculative balances in London working on the hypothesis of a return to gold at \$4.86 which would be withdrawn if expectations were not fulfilled, then one could argue that the Authorities, even if they did not return to gold, would have to take the same, or even stronger, measures to hold the exchange at \$4.80 as they would to return to gold. Such a choice of assumptions ruled out any consideration of the bulk of the exchange appreciation involved in returning to gold. In effect, this line of argument also obviated the need for analysing any specific adjustment problems connected with a return to gold in April 1925 as compared with, say, April 1927.

A final factor in 1925 and often thereafter, which heavily influenced policy discussions was what has since become known as the international role of sterling. Then, as often now, it was argued that the City and its institutions deserved special consideration on balance in the formulation of policy because invisible earnings played a large role in the balance of payments and because this role at the same time prevented conflicts between the City's interests and the national interest. As noted above,[27] hints of this approach were a part of the argument, particularly in the eyes of Niemeyer and Norman, for a return to gold in 1925 and after 1925 they played a considerable part in Keynes' rejection of devaluation as an alternative prior to August 1931.[28] In other circumstances, the argument was often implicit when phrases such as 'the national credit' found use as justifications for policy.[29] The argument has also found use in some *ex post* justifications of the policy actually chosen in 1925.[30] This approach to the position of the City, in my opinion, fundamentally confused two issues: the fact that sterling had an international role and the means through which such a role developed and was maintained. The international role of sterling some have argued might ' be better called an accident',[31] but economic theory provides some justification: the key in this case lying in the theory of portfolio selection.[32]

Individuals whose income or expenditure streams include foreign currency elements will tend to hold some foreign balances, if only to save on conversion costs. The exact size of these balances will, in addition, depend on the amount of these costs, relative interest rates and the volume of transactions.[33] This does not account for holdings of one particular foreign currency. However, the economies of pooling income and expenditure streams in several currencies into transactions in one vehicle currency to further reduce transactions costs and decrease the size of working balances provides a partial explanation. In addition elements of risk and return will induce holdings of foreign currencies over and above working balances, for an economic unit's country of residence is not necessarily the country in which it wishes to dispose of its wealth. The accumulation of assets in foreign currencies saves future asset exchange costs and also provides a hedge against future changes in the real value of wealth. Now where a country looms large in world trade, its currency will tend to be demanded for both transactions and asset-accumulation purposes. Even if wealth owners are uncertain as to their future commodity consumption patterns, the country offering the widest range of goods and services provides a useful first approximation to their possible future needs, subject to the principle of diversification to minimise risk. If this large trading country's currency possesses certain other advantages, over and above reductions in transactions costs resulting from the large volume of its foreign trade, it will tend to be still more favoured. If its financial markets are extensive, risk-averting investors will prefer it, for the probabilities of loss resulting from asset sales of a given size are lower than in a smaller market. If, in addition, its currency is not expected to fluctuate wildly or to depreciate in the long run, it will be preferred to other markets where this expectation is somewhat stronger.

This approach goes far to suggest why sterling developed as a vehicle and a reserve currency prior to 1914. The roots of development lay in Britain's trading position, her Empire, her policy of free trade and her dominance in world shipping and commodity transactions. To that base, over time she had evolved a financial system providing asset holders with a wide variety of assets, all easily traded in extensive markets, banking links into the domestic currency arrangements of many countries and a currency which was never scarce. Lastly, London's role as the major international capital market and almost a century of currency stability aided this process.

Given this background to the sterling system, the question arises as to whether the choice of an exchange rate other than $4.86 would have greatly affected London's position. The War left the basic institutions of the system largely unchanged. Six years of fluctuating exchanges and almost ten years of inconvertibility of various types had interposed themselves between the pre-war system and any successor. This instability and inconvertibility had removed one advantage of London as an international financial centre and had probably

86

contributed to the rise of New York. In this situation, any exchange rate, so long as it was destined to be stable, would probably have served London's purposes. The British financial system was stable and Government finance was conducted by exemplary standards from the contemporary point of view. Thus a lower parity for sterling would probably not have triggered off expectations that Britain would follow Germany or France, despite the frequency with which that bogey saw use in official presentations. From a longer term point of view, and even in the short term, a lower parity for sterling would have eased the City's position. Such a rate would have strengthened the underlying position of British industry in the international economy and made many services, such as shipping, more competitive. As noted above[34] a lower rate for sterling would not have weakened London's position in other areas of invisibles other than Government account. It probably would have increased the surplus on income account and hence eased the balance of payments problems that led to restrictions on certain types of transactions which affected London's international position. On a longer term basis, it would probably have strengthened the real forces underlying Britain's international banking role by strengthening the forces beneath Britain's long-term growth. For ultimately, the role of London as a financial centre depended on the underlying strength of the economy, not the reverse. Invisible earnings were large, but they were not a source of growth without a strong home economy which would allow unimpeded investment and intermediation.

However, as the adjustment problems were minimised by Churchill's advisers, the question of a rate for sterling other than $4.86 was never a live issue. Churchill, to a considerable extent, questioned many of his advisers' assumptions as to goals, but he was in a difficult situation, for intellectually he could see no alternative to a policy of drift,[35] and politically he had to rely on support in official circles, the City, business and the country which was almost unanimous in its desire for the policy actually chosen. Even the F.B.I., which might be regarded as one of the strongest critics of the details of the policy, both before and after April 1925, could see no alternative to drift, for it was committed to a return to gold, even at some discomfort to itself in the short-run, and regarded 'managed money' as only a stop gap.[36] The F.B.I. may not have been as fervent advocates of gold in 1925 as Professor Sayers suggests,[37] but it desired an end to uncertainty and admitted that 'considerations of high finance might make it so important that we should have to take the risk'.[38] Thus Churchill really had little alternative but to accept the advice generally offered, shortsighted though it was, and to adopt the gold standard at $4.86.

In fact, the decision-making style of the Authorities at the time is one of the most interesting aspects of the return to gold. Despite the amount of ink spilled in the course of the year before the decision, it can hardly be said that the decision was 'an exceptionally well-considered step'[39] when so little attention was actually given to the analysis of the existing situation. For a decision as to a rate of exchange not to involve a consideration of the current account implications of the step under consideration in relation to official policy goals seems almost foolhardy, as does the completely innumerate nature of the process.

Similarly, although the tendency to ignore the adjustment problem, given the lack of analysis of the underlying situation and the expectations of those involved is understandable to a considerable extent, it is still rather amazing. Churchill's memoranda had phrased the problems involved in a manner that cried out for analysis, but neither he nor anyone else really demanded it. Perhaps, the best explanation of the non-analytical nature of the decision-making process lies in the long run nature of most thinking at the time. Time and again in Niemeyer's briefs, the emphasis is on the long term: time and again this emphasis is used to circumvent short-term problems raised by Churchill. This long-term emphasis, plus an implicit belief that exchange rates once fixed were immutable,* probably contributed heavily to the analysis. Once this was accepted, the actual exchange rate chosen did not matter, for in the long run the system would adjust and adjust successfully. However, other than Keynes and McKenna, no one really attempted to point out just how long the short run might be.[†] One expects qualitative judgements ultimately to rule the roost in the formulation of economic policy — but for such judgements to dominate a policy decision, particularly when combined with an absolute minimum of analysis of its implications is most alarming.

From almost every point of view the decision was unfortunate and, despite all the emphasis on the long run, represented a triumph of short-term interests and conventional assumptions over long-term considerations and hard analysis. A lower exchange rate would not have solved all of the problems of the inter-war British economy, far from it. Such a rate might well, as Pigou argued later, have carried with it some increase in money wages, but such an increase would have been more a function of labour market conditions than exchange policy as such.[40][‡] A lower exchange rate, if adopted in the absence of a co-ordinated European stabilisation programme, might also have influenced the French and the Belgians to adopt even lower exchange rates than they actually did, an argument used by

---

* Devaluation or depreciation in cold blood without a prolonged struggle was unthinkable in the 1920's. In France, for example, although the franc had depreciated to $\frac{1}{5}$ of its pre-war exchange value, there was still significant segment of opinion which inclined to the view that appreciation to pre-war par was possible and desirable. (Moreau, *op. cit.*, 29 April–12 May, 1927.) In England, this feeling of immutability, based on almost 100 years experience before 1914 had its effects, for if one is setting rates for such a period 5 years' difficulties present no problems. In 1930–31 this consideration was certainly of some moment. (Keynes Papers, Macmillan Committee, Notes of Discussions, 7 November, 1930, 19–20.)

† Moreover, Keynes' and McKenna's expectations of inflation and their ambiguity in sorting out short-run problems from this longer term phenomenon weakened the impact of their advice considerably.

‡ Particularly given the decline in the popularity of cost-of-living adjusted wage agreements after 1920–22.

some observers to partially 'justify' $4.86.[41] Such an outcome was a possibility, but it assumes that the French and the Belgian exchange policies depended almost exclusively on the sterling exchange rate, or, to put it another way, that France and Belgium would make the same error as the British and completely ignore the multilateral aspects of exchange rate choices. It also assumes, that the somewhat healthier British economy, which one would assume would have resulted from a somewhat lower exchange rate which would have allowed greater concentration of fundamental problems in more buoyant conditions, would have been as seriously affected by possible French and Belgian decisions as a sickly one. Both of these assumptions seem tenous, to say the least. Similarly the suggestion that $4.40, or any other rate, might not have withstood the slump and 1931 does not damn alternative rates out of hand.[42] Exchange rates are not immutable things and long-term risks such as world slumps and massive liquidity crises cannot, to any great extent, be foreseen. Similarly a different exchange rate in 1925 would not have greatly altered the underlying positions of Germany and Central Europe or the problems of war debts. However it would have had two effects on the U.K., in addition to those arising from any movement towards greater international stability: first, she would have entered any subsequent difficulties after a period of relatively faster growth and with a stronger balance of payments; second, she would have entered these difficulties in a position where every British initiative to ease the situation did not look as if it was an attempt to shift the burden of adjustment, largely resulting from 1925, abroad.[43] The removal of this obstacle might have been important in such areas as the Kindersley Plan.[44] Such initiatives might not have saved the inter-war gold standard, but they perhaps would have paved the way for a more gradual and orderly transition of the international order and prevented the reaction and disintegration of the 1930s.

However, this is somewhat idle speculation. The basic point is that on the 1925 decision hung possibilities available to the decision makers at the time which those in authority missed. Having missed these possibilities, after 1925 they never really came to terms with making the alternative situation work successfully, largely because, as before 28 April, 1925, they paid very little attention to the existing situation and underlying trends. The return to gold, in many ways, represented one of the last attempts to apply simple conventional principles to financial and economic problems with a minimum of analysis. The decision and its supposed results largely represented a leap of faith for those involved. By its proponents, the return to gold at $4.86 was seen as an attempt to 'solve' several problems with one instrument. True this instrument was not supposed to 'solve' all problems, but it was to be an employment policy, a stabilisation policy, both national and international, 'of sorts', and an exchange policy. It was assumed that once this policy came into force, the traditional instruments of central bank policy, as refined since 1918, could deal with most other problems. Thus the gold standard plus Bank Rate could, for example, deal with the regulation of capital movements, both long- and short-term, the balance of trade, and, to some extent, the internal economy. This desire for simplicity, for 'a governor', for laissez faire, for 'a lost social automism',[45] had its last full fling as an instrument of policy in the gold standard as envisaged in 1925. Free trade, that other pillar of orthodoxy, by 1925 had been compromised by the McKenna Duties and the Safeguarding of Industries Act, both of which were reintroduced, after lapsing under the 1924 Labour Government, simultaneously with the return to gold. Even before 1931 the old simplicity seemed to be dying. Keynes' attitudes were, in many ways, symbolic of the changes occurring when in his replies to a series of questions addressed to members of the Economic Advisory Council he noted in July 1930:[46]

> 'All the same I am afraid of "principle". Ever since 1918 we, alone amongst the nations of the world, have been the slaves of "sound" general principles regardless of particular circumstances. We have behaved as though the intermediate "short periods" of the economist between our [one?] position of equilibrium and another were short, whereas they can be long enough — and have been before now — to encompass the decline and downfall of nations. Nearly all our difficulties have been traceable to an unaltering service to the principles of "sound finance" which all our neighbours have neglected.

> 'This "long run" policy is a grand thing in its way — unless, like the operators of systems at Monte Carlo, one has not enough resources to last through the short run. Wasn't it Lord Melbourne who said that "No statesman ever does anything really foolish except on principle."?

> . . .

> 'When we come to the question of remedies for the local situation as distinct from the international, the peculiarity of my position lies, perhaps in the fact that I am in favour of practically all the remedies which have been suggested in any quarter. Some of them are better than others. But nearly all of them seem to me to tend in the right direction. The unforgiveable attitude is, therefore for me the negative one, — the repelling of each of these remedies in turn.

> 'Accordingly, I favour an eclectic programme, making use of suggestions from all quarters, not expecting too much from the application of any one of them, but hoping that they may do something in the aggregate.'

Have things changed that greatly since?

Appendix

Chapter III briefly discussed the goals of the Authorities with respect to foreign investment, trade and employment. At that time, no attempt was made to attach very precise estimates as to the effects of appreciating the exchange to $4.86 on these goals. Below some 'back of an envelope' estimates provide a rough indication of the orders of magnitude of the changes in the components of the current account balance involved in the appreciation of sterling from around $4.40 to $4.86 in 1924–25 and the implications of these for the policy goals of the Authorities. Throughout the discussion, the alternative exchange rate assumed is approximately 10 per cent below $4.86. Such a rate is plausible both from the 1924 exchange position and from the implications arising from the discussion of purchasing-power parity estimates and of changes in Britain's international economic position from that of a typical pre-war year in Chapter III.

The discussion will proceed in two stages with: (1) an indication of the impact effects, *ceteris paribus*, of the appreciation of the exchange rate by 11 per cent between 1924 and 1925, and (2) an indication of the implications of an exchange rate 10 per cent below $4.86 in a typical post-1925 year. In both cases, the impact effects of the changes on the balance of payments will be compared to those resulting from other developments or policy changes.

Both calculations, for their estimates of the effects of changes in exchange rates on the trade account, take advantage of the numerous estimates of the price elasticities of demand for exports and imports made since the 1930s, with full knowledge of all the difficulties involved.[1] For the present calculations, imports of goods are assumed to have a sterling price elasticity of demand of –0.5 (i.e. a one per cent fall in the sterling price of imports relative to other goods will raise the volume of imports demanded by 0.5 per cent) and exports of goods are assumed to have a foreign currency price elasticity of demand –1.5.* Throughout the calculations which follow, unless otherwise stated, all reckoning is done in sterling.

Effects of the Appreciation of Sterling in 1924–25

Assuming that all other things remain equal (employment, world demand,

---

* Both of these assumptions are, if anything, conservative in that they lie towards the lower end of the range suggested in the literature. This choice of conservative values will minimise the balance of payments effects of exchange rate changes.

foreigners' prices in third markets, etc.) an estimate of the impact effects of an 11 per cent appreciation in the exchange value of sterling between 1924 and 1925 is possible. The 1924 current account figures (exports of U.K. produce, £801 million; retained imports, £1137 million; and invisible surplus, £409 million) provide a rough base on which to build the estimates.* Assuming that the appreciation resulted in some reduction in import prices which benefitted exporters and that exporters narrowed their profit margins in the face of increased foreign competition, export prices in foreign currency would rise by, say, 7 per cent as a result of appreciation. On the import side, assuming that foreigners took the opportunity to raise profit margins, prices in sterling would fall by 8 per cent. Given these changes in relative prices and using the elasticities given above, the implications for exports and imports are as follows:

	Exports	Imports
Percentage change in volume	− 10.5	+ 4.0
Percentage change in sterling value	− 14.1	− 4.3
Change from 1924 level in £ million	−112.9	−48.9

Thus on trade account, on the above assumptions, the appreciation of sterling by 11 per cent would imply a worsening of the trade deficit by £64 million.

On invisible account, as noted in Chapter III, appreciation would result in divergent movements. Reckoning again in sterling, net shipping earnings could be expected to fall as foreign operators' costs fell relative to U.K.; net income from short interest and commissions would fall as foreigners needed a smaller sterling amount to cover a foreign currency transaction of a given size and as the U.K. was a net exporter of such services; net income on overseas debt investment would remain unchanged as both debits and credits were predominantly denominated in sterling; net income on overseas equity investment would fall as credits were determined in foreign currencies by foreign conditions and debits were determined in sterling by U.K. conditions; net tourism earnings would remain roughly unchanged, as would other private invisibles; and net Government expenditure on war debts and other items would fall. As the major expenditure item to fall would be on Government account and would only be of the order of, say, £5 million; whereas, the income falls, particularly given that almost 30 per cent of U.K. overseas investment was in equity form which provided yields about 1½ times those of debt investment,[2] would extend over a much larger area, in all probability the adverse change in the invisible account would be substantial, of the order of at least £15 million if one makes another conservative estimate.

Thus, on the 1924 current account figures, one would expect, *ceteris paribus,*

---

* Rough, if only because the range of exchange movements in 1924 certainly affected the 1924 figures, making them only partially indicative of the implications of a stable exchange rate of approximately $4.38.

that the balance of payments on current account would deteriorate by roughly £80 million (1924 surplus = £73 million) as a result of the impact effects of an 11 per cent appreciation in the sterling exchange. This would have meant a deficit on current account of roughly £7 million, to be considered in conjunction with new overseas issues of long-term capital of approximately £100 million.

To relieve the resulting strain on the balance of payments, the Authorities would have several possibilities open:*

(a) They could reduce employment and national income by an amount necessary to provide sufficient relief to allow the attainment of other goals. Each reduction in employment of 1000 men, given net national income per person employed of £185.6[3] and a marginal propensity to import of 0.3,[4] could be expected to reduce imports by £55,680. To offset the whole effect of appreciation on the current account in this way would have meant adding 1.4 million to the existing number unemployed. Each reduction in employment would, moreover, imply moving further from the pseudo-full employment goal at a time when unemployment was over 10 per cent.

(b) They could hope that rises in overseas costs relative to U.K. costs would, through their effects on relative prices, increase U.K. exports and reduce imports. This could occur through exchange appreciations or inflationary developments abroad, the latter of course being commonly expected at the time of the return to gold. Each 1 per cent rise in foreign costs relative to U.K. costs, if fully passed on in foreign prices, would imply a 0.5 per cent rise in the sterling value of imports of goods (i.e. about £5.4 million, if one works from the 1924 trade figures adjusted for the effects of appreciation) and a 1.5 per cent rise in the sterling value of exports of goods (i.e. about £10.3 million).[†] This implies that a relative rise of overseas costs of about 15 per cent would have been necessary to offset the full current account effects of appreciation. Of course, any declines in relative costs abroad, resulting from exchange depreciations, deflationary developments or unfavourable changes in wages and productivity, would have adverse effects.

(c) They could hope that the terms of trade would turn in the U.K.'s favour through a decline in the prices of non-competing imports, which would reduce the import bill. A fall of about 10 per cent in these prices, with export prices unchanged, would be needed to restore the *ex ante* current account surplus — provided one can ignore the effects of such a fall on U.K. exports.

(d) They could hope that any increase in unemployment generated in (a) would reduce U.K. money wages (or hold them stable while foreign money wages rose) and that this, plus divergent rates of productivity growth would reduce

---

* Each of these is considered *ceteris paribus*.

† Using the elasticity estimates given above and assuming no changes in foreigners' profit margins or U.K. export prices in sterling.

sterling wage costs per unit of output, thus making U.K. exports and import competing goods cheaper relative to foreign goods so that (b) could operate.

(e) They could reduce overseas lending by intensifying controls on lending abroad by U.K. residents. Although this would mean some slight decline in U.K. exports, it would improve the overall balance of payments position. However, a reduction of over £80 million in overseas lending would virtually mean ending all foreign issues in London and giving up one of the Authorities' policy goals.*

(f) They could through increased protection reduce imports, although this would also imply giving up the free trade goal.

(g) They could hope that a rise in world import demand for goods and services would raise U.K. exports despite the latter's high relative costs. A 10 per cent increase in world demand for imported goods would raise the demand for U.K. exports by £69 million, all other things remaining equal.

This list by no means exhausts all of the possibilities, which could be combined in various ways, for improving the balance of payments position and offsetting the deterioration implicit in the appreciation of the exchange between 1924 and 1925. Each of the calculations above, although made under restrictive assumptions which largely ignore repercusion effects, merely presents in a simple form, an order of magnitude for each possibility. In 1924—25, the Authorities hoped that (b) and (g) would bear the primary burden in the ensuing adjustment process, and that (a), (e) and (d) would play a subsidiary role. However, given the general tendency throughout the discussions to avoid specifics and quantification, there was never any attempt to foresee exactly what burden the return to gold at $4.86 imposed on the adjustment mechanism. As a result, the Authorities ultimately gave up, in varying degrees, all of their goals in the hope, which analysis indicates was somewhat specious, that $4.86 rather than an equally stable lower rate would increase London's invisible earnings and that the adjustment mechanism would so operate as to allow the achievement of other goals.

The Alternative Position in a Typical Post-1925 Year

Taking 1928 as a typical post-1925 year, one can also examine, in a similar manner, the balance of payments implications of an exchange rate 10 per cent below $4.86. 1928 provides a useful post-1925 year, because by that time most other currencies had been stabilised for a sufficiently long period to allow their effects to be felt, and on the realised British data it is a year relatively free from the disruptions of the General Strike and its aftermath and from the effects of the later depression. Under these conditions, it is worthwhile to take a rather

---

* New foreign issues in 1924—25 averaged £111 million.

94

timeless* look at the effects of an exchange rate 10 per cent below $4.86 using the British 1928 current account figures.†

Assume that if sterling had been at $4.38 in 1928 export prices for U.K. goods in foreign currencies would have been 6 per cent below their 1928 levels, the remaining effects of the lower exchange rate showing themselves in higher costs resulting from increased import prices and higher profit margins which would raise sterling prices. Similarly assume that sterling import prices would have been 9 per cent above their 1928 levels, allowing for some narrowing of profit margins. Using the same elasticities as above, on the goods side the import and export position would have appeared, *ceteris paribus*, as follows:

	Exports	Imports
Percentage change in volume	+ 9.0	– 4.5
Percentage change in sterling value	+13.3	+ 4.1
Change from 1928 level in £ million	+96.2	+44.1

This results in an improvement in the balance of trade of £52.1 million. If arguing on the same lines as previously, one allows for an improvement in the invisible account of, say, £15 million, the overall improvement approaches £70 million.

This relief on the balance on current account could have been used in various ways. For example:

(a) The Authorities could have achieved a higher level of employment without sacrificing other goals. In 1928, unemployment averaged 10.8 per cent, or 1,290,000. If it had stood at the pseudo-full employment level of 4.7 per cent, or 561,000 and if the remaining 729,000 men had found jobs and produced the national average net domestic income per person employed of £191.3,[5] assuming again a marginal propensity to import of 0.3, the additional imports of £41.8 million could easily have been contained by the improvement in the trade balance resulting from this 'timeless' calculation of the implications of an exchange rate of $4.38. At the same time, a margin of over £25 million would be left for other objectives. Thus, if wages had not risen, or if productivity had risen by an additional amount over the trend rate sufficient to enable some wage increases without raising unit costs, a lower exchange

---

* Timeless because the analysis ignores the effects on the U.K. of an extended period at a lower exchange rate in terms of growth and of the possibility of avoiding the disruptions of 1925–26. In fact, this part of the exercise might better be considered as an exercise in estimating the effects of devaluation in 1928.

† Retained imports, £1,076 million; exports of U.K. produce, £724 million; surplus on invisibles, £475 million.

rate would have allowed* the Authorities something approaching their goal and even have left some room for increased net foreign lending.

(b) Alternatively, the Authorities could have relaxed controls on foreign lending. The appropriate no-control level of overseas lending is probably impossible to estimate, given the rise of the United States as a lender and its increasing dominance in areas such as Latin America and Canada and other changes in the international economy. However, given the improvement in the current account postulated above and adding this to the 1928 surplus of £123 million, the possibilities for net foreign lending open to the U.K. exceed £190 million. Even allowing for the effects of a higher level of employment postulated in (a) above, the additional lending possible would have implied a higher level of net foreign lending than occurred at any time during the 1920s.

This list of possibilities could be extended in several directions — reserve accumulation, freer trade, etc. — but the basic outlines are clear. The return to gold in 1925 at $4.86, as compared with a return to gold at $4.38 with conservativ assumptions as to price elasticities of demand for imports and exports of goods and the impact of exchange rate changes on invisibles, to name only two, removed from the Authorities' grasp the possibility of achieving certain goals. The two sets of calculations do not 'prove' anything as to the full extent of the possibilities foregone, but they do provide useful additional criteria for an informed judgement as to the implications of a return to gold at $4.86 and provide a rough check on the hypothesis that 10 per cent would provide a reasonable first approximation to the extent of sterling's overvaluation in 1925 in relation to the policy goals of the Authorities.

---

* I use the term allow deliberately, for a changed exchange value for sterling would not necessarily ensure that pseudo-full employment came to pass, although it would have created pressures operating in the right direction.

References

The following abbreviations have found use when papers are used:

1. F.R.B.N.Y. – Federal Reserve Bank of New York Archives.

2. Public Record Office materials. Here footnotes refer only to the call numbers for the documents concerned (e.g. TI72/1499B). The full titles and call numbers for the files that have found use are:

Cab. 58 – Cabinet Office. Economic Advisory Council (Committee of Civil Research).

   Cab. 58/2, Economic Advisory Council, Minutes, 17 February, 1930 – 15 January, 1932.

   Cab. 58/9, Committee of Civil Research, Memoranda, (H) Series, Nos. 1–50, 29 June, 1925–18 March, 1925.

   Cab. 58/11, Economic Advisory Council, Memoranda, (H) Series, Nos. 101–130, 16 July, 1930–19 November, 1930.

T160 – Treasury. Finance Files.

   T160/197/F7528, Committee on the Currency and Bank of England Note Issues.

T160/197/F7528/01/1–3, Chamberlain–Bradbury Committee on Gold Standard and Amalgamation of Treasury Note Issues with Bank of England Note Issue: Proceedings.

   T160/197/F7528/03, Return to the Gold Standard in U.K. Press Cuttings.

   T160/463/F8362/1, Return to the Gold Standard.

   T160/227/F8508, Revolving Credit for the United Kingdom ($300,000,000) for a period of two years.

T170 – Treasury. Bradbury Papers.

   T170/129, The Regulation of the Exchanges and of Gold Export, 1918.

T172 – Treasury. Chancellor of the Exchequer's Office: Miscellaneous Papers.

   T172/1499B, Gold Standard 1925: Treasury Memoranda.

   T172/1500A, Gold Standard 1925: American Credits.

T175 – Treasury. Hopkins Papers.

T175/9, Proposed Return to the Gold Standard, 1925.

T175/11, Financial and Industrial Situations in Great Britain and Germany, 1927.

T175/46, B.I.S. Gold Guarantee, 1931.

T175/56, General Financial Policy, 1931–32.

T176 – Treasury, Neimeyer Papers.

T176/5, Monetary Policy, 1920–1929.

T176/13, Bank Rate, 1923–1930.

T176/16, Gold Standard, 1925.

T176/22, Internal Gold Circulation, 1925–27.

All numbers not preceded by 'Ch.' or 'para.', or otherwise indentified, are page references.

Chapter I

1. J.M. Keynes, *The Economic Consequences of Mr. Churchill*, (London, 1925), 27–31.

2. Keynes Papers, Letter to J.R. MacDonald, 5 August, 1931.

3. Committee on Finance and Industry, *Report*, Cmd. 3897, (London, 1931), para. 255–7; Addendum I, para. 32–3.

4. Cab. 58/2, Economic Advisory Council, 13th Meeting, 16 April, 1931, 4.

5. R. Skidelsky, 'Crisis 1931', *The Times*, 4 December, 1968, 27. The same statement is attributed to Lord Passfield, again without noting its source, by A.J.P. Taylor, *English History 1914–1945*, (London, 1965), 297.

6. The classic expedient here is of course protection. For a full programme, see Keynes' presentation to the Macmillan Committee in its discussions of 20, 21, 28 February, 6 and 7 March, 1930. Keynes Papers.

7. L.V. Chandler, *Benjamin Strong, Central Banker*, (Washington, 1958), esp. Ch. VII and VIII.
Sir Henry Clay, *Lord Norman*, (London, 1957), esp. Ch. IV.
A. Boyle, *Montagu Norman*, (London 1967), esp. Ch. 7 and 8.

8. Sir F.W. Leith Ross, *Money Talks: Fifty Years of International Finance*, (London, 1968), Ch. 9,
Sir P.J. Grigg, *Prejudice and Judgement*, (London, 1948), esp. 182–93.

9. S.V.O. Clarke, *Central Bank Cooperation 1924–31*, (New York, 1967), Ch. 5.

10. R.S. Sayers, 'The Return to Gold 1925', L.S. Presnell ed., *Studies in the Industrial Revolution*, (London, 1960).

11. Clay, for example, knew of the two volumes of memoranda and cables discussed below but was refused access by Sir Norman Brook. The documents referred to are T172/1499B and T172/1500A.

12. Keynes, *op.cit.*, 11. Keynes used this figure as a minimum for in it he referred only to the dollar exchange while admitting that even at the lower 1924 rate sterling was overvalued in terms of the European exchanges. *Ibid.*, 8, 21, 32.

13. *Ibid.*, 8.

14. As told to Per Jacobsson, 8 May, 1932. E.E. Jucker-Fleetwood, 'Montagu Norman in the Per Jacobsson Diaries', *National Westminster Bank Quarterly Review*, November, 1968, 68.

15. Keynes, *Economic Consequences of Mr. Churchill*, 10.

16. *Ibid.*, 11–12.

17. P.J. Grigg, *op.cit.*, 182–4.

18. Committee on the Currency and Bank of England Note Issues, *Report*, Cmd. 2393, (London, 1925).

19. For a thorough discussion see F.W. Fetter, *The Development of British Monetary Orthodoxy 1797–1875*, (Cambridge, 1965), Ch. II–IV.

20. E.V. Morgan, *Studies in British Financial Policy 1914–25*, (London, 1952), 356.

21. Committee on Currency and Foreign Exchanges After the War, *Report*, Cmd. 464, (London, 1919), 2. The terms of reference were later extended to include the words 'and to consider the working of the Bank Act, 1844, and the constitution and functions of the Bank of England with a view to recommending any alterations which may appear to them to be necessary or desirable'.

22. This *Interim Report* was made public in November 1918.

23. Committee on Currency and Foreign Exchanges After the War, *First Interim Report*, Cd. 9182, (London, 1918), para. 1.

24. *Ibid.*, para. 15.

25. Clay, *op.cit.*, 112.

26. Cunliffe Committee, *First Interim Report*, para. 47.

27. 2 November, 1918, 618–19. See also L.J. Hume, 'The Gold Standard and

Deflation: Issues and Attitudes in the Nineteen-Twenties', *Economica*, N.S., XXX(3), August 1963, 228 ff.

28. Cd. 9227, (London, 1918).

29. Cunliffe Committee, *First Interim Report*, para. 14.

30. Clay, *op.cit.*, 116.

31. A.C. Pigou, *Aspects of British Economic History 1918—25*, (London, 1947), 146.

32. T170/129, J.M. Keynes to Sir John Bradbury, 4 January, 1919. This document is dated January 1918 in the files, but internal evidence, particularly its use of exchange quotations for 30 December, 1918 indicates a January 1919 date.

33. *Ibid.*, 3.

34. *Ibid.*, 2 and 5.

35. Clay, *op.cit.*, 116—117

36. Boyle, *op.cit.*, 126.

37. For a good discussion of all these steps see W.A. Brown Jr., *The International Gold Standard Reinterpreted 1914—1934*, Vol.I, (New York, 1940), 177—190.

38. T176/5, O.E. Niemeyer, 'Memorandum on Deflation', undated but its position in the file suggests the summer of 1921.

39. For a thorough discussion of the 1918—19 position see Morgan, *op.cit.*, 114—15, 138—56, 202—7; Clay, *op.cit.*, 109—134.

40. B.R. Mitchell and P. Deane, *Abstract of British Historical Statistics*, (Cambridge 1962), Public Finance 3 and 4.

41. Pember and Boyle, *British Government Securities in the Twentieth Century*, 2nd ed., (London, 1950), 395, 401.

42. Macmillan Committee, *Report*, Appendix I.

43. Pigou, *op.cit.*, 158—9.

44. Sir John Clapham, *The Bank of England*, Vol. II, (New York, 1945), 421—2

45. The phrase is Professor Pigou's (*op.cit.*, 7).

46. London and Cambridge Economic Service, *The British Economy, Key Statistics 1900—66*, (London, n.d.), Table B.

47. G. Routh, *Occupation and Pay in Great Britain 1906—60*, (Cambridge, 1965), 114—5.

48. London and Cambridge Economic Service, *op.cit.*, Table B.

49. J.M. Keynes, *A Tract on Monetary Reform*, (London, 1923), 195.

50. Clay, *op.cit.*, 140.

51. *Ibid.*, 145–6. T176/13, Niemeyer to Norman, 23 June, 1923.

52. F.R.B.N.Y., Norman to Strong, 21 March, 1922; Clay, *op.cit.*, 141.

53. Clay, *op.cit.*, 173–210.

54. *Ibid.*, 143.

55. *Ibid.*, 146–148. T176/5, Niemeyer to Chancellor, undated but internal evidence indicates 1923; T176/13, Niemeyer to Norman, 23 June, 1923; T176/5, R.G. Hawtrey, Memoranda 31 October and 17 November, 1923; Niemeyer to Norman, 20 November, 1923; Norman to Niemeyer, 21 November, 1923.

56. T176/5, Niemeyer to Chancellor, undated.

57. T176/5, R.G. Hawtrey, Memorandum, 31 October, 1923.

58. T176/5, Norman to Niemeyer, 21 November, 1923.

59. Clay, *op.cit.*, 148.

60. K.S. Lomax, 'Production and Productivity Movements in the United Kingdom Since 1900'. *Journal of the Royal Statistical Society*, Series A, CXXII(2), 1959, 192–3.

61. London and Cambridge Economic Service, *op.cit.*, Table E.

62. Pigou, *op.cit.*, Statistical Appendix, Section I, Table VI.

63. *Ibid.*, Statistical Appendix, Section I, Table IX.

64. Ministry of Labour, *Eighteenth Abstract of Labour Statistics of the United Kingdom*, Cmd. 2740, (London, 1926), 70–73.

65. Routh, *op.cit.*, 109–15; Pigou, *op.cit.*, 48–52, 206–7.

66. London and Cambridge Economic Service, *op.cit.*, Table B.

67. *Ibid.*, Table K; I. Svennilson, *Growth and Stagnation in the European Economy*, (Geneva, 1954), Table A58.

68. Mitchell and Deane, *op.cit.*, Iron and Steel 9 and 10.

69. *Ibid.*, Textiles 4.

70. *Ibid.*, Coal 5.

71. *Ibid.*, Transport 2; Board of Trade, *Statistical Abstract for the United Kingdom 1913–33*, Cmd. 4801, (London, 1935), Table 227.

72. Morgan, *op.cit.*, 342–3.

73. O.T. Falk, 'Currency and Gold: Now and after the War', *Economic Journal*,

XXVII (109), March 1918, 49.

74.   Morgan, *op.cit.*, 330—31.

75.   If anything, this estimate may be a bit low. Royal Institute of International Affairs, *The Problem of International Investment*, (London, 1965), 160.

76.   For some discussion of London's 1913 position see: Morgan, *op.cit.*, 332, 343; A.I. Bloomfield, *Short-Term Capital Movements under the Pre-1914 Gold Standard*, (Princeton, 1963), 66, 76; P.M. Oppenheimer, 'Monetary Movements and the International Position of Sterling', *Scottish Journal of Political Economy*, XIII(1), February 1966, 92—5.

77.   Morgan, *op.cit.*, 342—343.

78.   Mitchell and Deane, *op.cit.*, Transport 1.

79.   B. Thomas, 'The Historical Record of International Capital Movements', J.H. Adler ed., *Capital Movements and Economic Development*, (London, 1967), 15.

80.   T. Balogh, *Studies in Financial Organisation*, (Cambridge, 1947), 244—5 indicates that rates for acceptances actually fell.

81.   Mitchell and Deane, *op.cit.*, Transport 4.

82.   Royal Institute of International Affairs, *op.cit.*, 131.

83.   London and Cambridge Economic Service, *op.cit.*, Table K.

84.   S.B. Saul, *Studies in British Overseas Trade 1870—1914*, (Liverpool, 1960) Ch. III.

85.   Balogh, *op.cit.*, 174

86.   *Ibid.*, 165—68.

87.   T175/46, Treasury Bill Figures, undated.

88.   Committee on Finance and Industry, *Minutes of Evidence*, (London 1931), Q.1147, 1159; Balogh, *op.cit.*, 233—34.

89.   Brown, *op.cit.*, 652—3, 666, Committee on Finance and Industry, *Evidence*, Q.1273.

Chapter II

1.   Clay, *op.cit.*, 149.

2.   T160/197/F7528, Norman to Niemeyer, 16 April, 1924.

3.   *First Interim Report*, para. 41, 47.

4.   T160/197/F7528, Norman to Niemeyer, 16 April, 1924.

5.   T160/197/F7528, Niemeyer to Fisher and Chancellor, 5 May, 1924. This

note is dated 5/4/24, but as it appears in a file opened 16/4/24 and as it attached Norman's letter of that date, it seems likely that the data should be 5/5/24. T160/197/F7528, Niemeyer to Chancellor, 19 May, 1924.

6. Treasury Minute, 10 June, 1924.

7. Pigou Papers, Committee on the Currency and Bank of England Note Issues, Minutes of First Meeting.

8. J.M. Keynes, 'Notes and Memoranda. The Committee on the Currency', *Economic Journal*, XXXV(138), June 1925, 229; E. Cannan, 'Review of T.E. Gregory, *The Return to Gold*', *Economic Journal*, XXXV(140); December, 1925, 615; See below.

9. Clay, *op.cit.*, 149.

10. Pigou Papers, *op.cit.*, Evidence of M.C. Norman, 1–2.

11. *Ibid.*, 2–3.

12. *Ibid.*, 7.

13. *Ibid.*, 6–7.

14. *Ibid.*, 10.

15. *Ibid.*, 9.

16. *Ibid.*, 10.

17. *Ibid.*, 14.

18. *Ibid.*, 16.

19. *Ibid.*, 11.

20. *Ibid.*, 19.

21. *Ibid.*, 11–12.

22. *Ibid.*, 17.

23. *Ibid.*, 13.

24. *Ibid.*, 19.

25. Clay, *op.cit.*, 138.

26. Pigou Papers, *op.cit.*, Evidence of Sir Charles Addis, 58–9.

27. *Ibid.*, 60.

28. *Ibid.*, 45.

29. *Ibid.*, 44–45, 57–58.

30. *Ibid.*, 45.

31. *Ibid.*, 45–6.

32. *Ibid.*, 45–6.

33. Pigou Papers, *op.cit.*, Evidence of J.M. Keynes, 15.

34. *Ibid.*, 4.

35. *Ibid.*, 14.

36. *Ibid.*, 14.

37. *Ibid.*, 16.

38. *Ibid.*, 16, 23.

39. *Ibid.*, 18–19; See also J.M. Keynes, *Tract on Monetary Reform*, (London, 1923), 174–6.

40. Pigou Papers, *op.cit.*, Evidence of J.M. Keynes, 16–17.

41. Pigou Papers, *op.cit.*, Evidence of R. McKenna, 1, 21.

42. *Ibid.*, 24.

43. *Ibid.*, 26.

44. *Ibid.*, 11–12.

45. *Ibid.*, 21.

46. *Ibid.*, 12–13.

47. *Ibid.*, 14–15, 17.

48. *Ibid.*, 15–16.

49. *Ibid.*, 22–3.

50. Pigou Papers, *op.cit.*, Evidence of Professor E. Cannan, 5–6. See also evidence of Sir George Paish, 24.

51. *Ibid.*, 10.

52. *Ibid.*, 10.

53. *Ibid.*, 14, 34.

54. *Ibid.*, 19.

55. Pigou Papers, *op.cit.*, Evidence of W. Leaf, 4, 7.

56. *Ibid.*, 5.

57. *Ibid.*, 5.

58. Pigou Papers, *op.cit.*, Evidence of W. Leaf, 4, 7.

59. *Ibid.*, 3, 4, 18–19.

60. *Ibid.*, 3, 6.

61. *Ibid.*, 3.

62. Pigou Papers, *op.cit.*, Evidence of Sir R. Horne, 1; Evidence of Mr. Currie, 8–9, Evidence of Sir F. Schuster, 32; F.B.I. Statement, 1; Evidence of Messrs. Chisholm and Glenday, 1.

63. Pigou Papers, *op.cit.*, F.B.I. Statement, 4.

64. Pigou Papers, *op.cit.*, Evidence of Mr. Currie, 5; Evidence of Mr. Goodenough, 4, 20; Evidence of Sir R. Horne, 4; F.B.I. Statement, 2.

65. *Ibid.*, 3.

66. Pigou Papers, *op.cit.*, Evidence of Sir R. Horne, 6.

67. Pigou Papers, *op.cit.*, F.B.I. Statement, 3.

68. Pigou Papers, *op.cit.*, Evidence of Sir R. Horne.

69. Pigou Papers, *op.cit.*, Evidence of Mr. Currie, 4; Evidence of Sir W.H.N. Goschen, 6; Evidence of Sir F. Schuster, 13; Evidence of Mr. Goodenough, 4.

70. Pigou Papers, *op.cit.*, Evidence of Sir F. Schuster, 28–29; Evidence of Mr. Goodenough, 22.

71. Pigou Papers, *op.cit.*, Evidence of Messrs. Chisholm and Glenday, 11.

72. Pigou Papers, *op.cit.*, Evidence of Sir R. Horne, 17.

73. T160/197/F7528/01/1, Bradbury to Farrer, 24 July, 1924.

74. T160/187/F7528/01/1, Young to Chamberlain, 23 August, 1924; T160/197/F7528/01/2, Committee on the Currency and Bank of England Note Issues, Second Draft of Report.

75. *Ibid.*, para. 5.

76. *Ibid.*, para. 6.

77. *Ibid.*, para. 7–10.

78. *Ibid.*, para. 11.

79. *Ibid.*, para. 12.

80. *Ibid.*, para. 13–14.

81. *Ibid.*, para. 14.

82. T160/197/F7528/01/2, Bradbury to Young, 11 September, 1924.

83. T160/197/F7528/01/1, Farrer to Young, 24 August, 1924. T160/197/F7528/01/2, Chamberlain to Young, 11 and 13 September, 1924.

84. T160/197/F7528/01/2, quoted in Young to Bradbury, 12 September, 1924.

85. T160/197/F7528/01/2, Chamberlain to Young, 13 September, 1924.

86. *Ibid.*, T160/197/F7528/01/2, Young to Norman, 18 September, 1924.

87. T160/197/F7528/01/2, Committee on Currency and Bank of England Note Issues, Third Draft Report, 14 September, 1924, para. 8–9.

88. *Ibid.*, para. 11, 15, 18, 20–30.

89. *Ibid.*, para. 37.

90. F.R.B.N.Y., Strong Papers, Strong to Mellon, 27 May, 1924.

91. F.R.B.N.Y., Strong Papers, Strong to Jay, 23–28 April, 1924.

92. F.R.B.N.Y., Strong Papers, Strong to Norman, 3 June, 1924; E.R. Wicker, *Federal Reserve Monetary Policy 1917–33*, (New York, 1966) 83, 85, 89.

93. Clarke, *op.cit.*, 76 fn.

94. F.R.B.N.Y., Strong to Jay, 4 April, 1924.

95. F.R.B.N.Y., Norman to Strong, 16 June, 1924.

96. See above 26–27; F.R.B.N.Y., Norman to Strong, 16 June, 1924.

97. See for example, 'The Past Month', *Bankers' Magazine*, CXVIII(2) August 1924; 'Finance and Investment', *The Nation*, 28 June and 5 July, 1924.

98. Pigou Papers, *op.cit.*, Evidence of Mr. Leaf, 3.

99. *Ibid.*, 3, 13.

100. 'Finance and Investment', *The Nation*, 28 June, 1924.

101. 'Finance and Investment', *The Nation*, 8 November, 1924; *The Economist*, 3 January, 1925, 4.

102. F.R.B.N.Y., Norman to Strong, No. 95, 19 July, 1924.

103. F.R.B.N.Y., Strong Papers, Strong to Norman, 9 July, 1924.

104. F.R.B.N.Y., Strong Papers, Strong to Lubbock, 10 September, 1924.

105. F.R.B.N.Y., Strong Papers, Lubbock to Strong, 25 August, 1924.

106. Clay, *op.cit.*, 149–50.

107. F.R.B.N.Y., Strong Papers, Norman to Strong, 16 October, 1924.

108. F.R.B.N.Y., Strong Papers, Strong to Norman, 4 November, 1924.

109. Clay, *op.cit.*, 151.

110. Chandler, *op.cit.*, 308.

111. See below 62.

112. Boyle, *op.cit.*, 179.

113. Leith-Ross, *op.cit.*, 88, 118.

114. Boyle, *op.cit.*, 179.

115. Grigg, *op.cit.*, 174, 180.

116. T172/1500A, Norman to Niemeyer, 4 December, 1924.

117. Chartwell Papers, File 18/2, Churchill to Baldwin, 12 December, 1924.

118. F.R.B.N.Y., Strong Papers, Memorandum, 11 January, 1925.

119. *Ibid.*

120. *Ibid.*

121. *Ibid.*

122. Chandler, *op.cit.*, 313–16.

123. F.R.B.N.Y., Norman to Lubbock, No. 15, 6 January, 1925.

124. F.R.B.N.Y., Norman to Lubbock, No. 16, 6 January, 1925.

125. F.R.B.N.Y., Lubbock to Norman, Nos. 54, 55 and 57, 10 and 12 January, 1925.

126. T172/1500A, Niemeyer to Norman, 8 December, 1924; T175/9 Niemeyer to Lubbock, 9 January, 1925; T172/1500A, Fisher to Niemeyer, 12 January, 1925.

127. T160/197/F7528/01/2, Farrer to Young, 20 December, 1924.

128. F.R.B.N.Y., Strong Papers, Norman to Strong, 24 January, 1924.

129. T160/197/F7528/01/3, Committee on the Currency and Bank of England Note Issues, Fourth Draft Report, 26 January, 1925, Pigou Papers, *op.cit.*, Evidence of the Governor of the Bank of England and Sir Charles Addis, 1.

130. See below 44–5.

131. T160/197/F7528/01/3, Fourth Draft Report, 6–7.

132. *Ibid.*, 7–8.

133. *Ibid.*, 5–6.

134. Pigou Papers, *op.cit.*, Evidence of the Governor of the Bank of England and Sir Charles Addis, 1.

135. *Ibid.*, 2–3.

136. *Ibid.*, 4, 5.

137. *Ibid.*, 5–7, 11.

138. *Ibid.*, 7–8.

139. See below 58.

140. *Ibid.*, 10–11.

141. *Ibid.*, 31–2.

142. *Ibid.*, 39.

143. *Ibid.*, 18.

144. *Ibid.*, 16–22.

145. *Ibid.*, 18–19.

146. *Ibid.*, 22.

147. *Ibid.*, 28–39.

148. T160/197/F7528/01/3, Pigou to Young, undated. The revisions occur in what were paragraphs 19 and 20 of the published report.

149. F.R.B.N.Y., Norman to Strong, No. 67, 13 February, 1925.

150. In T172/1499B, Niemeyer's memorandum is undated but appears before the Churchill memorandum mentioned below. In T175/9, the Niemeyer memorandum, 'The Gold Export Prohibition' is dated 2 February, 1925 or after the Churchill Minute.

151. T175/9, Bradbury to Niemeyer, 5 February, 1925.

152. T172/1499B, 'Mr. Churchill's Exercise', 29 January, 1925.

153. Lord Salter, *Slave of the Lamp A Public Servant's Notebook*, (London, 1967), 248–50.

154. T172/1499B, 'The Gold Export Prohibition', 'Commentary', 2 February, 1925.

155. T172/1499B, 2 February, 1925.

156. T172/1499B, 'The Gold Standard', 5 February, 1925.

157. T172/1499B, 'The Gold Standard', 2 February, 1925.

158. T172/1499B, Churchill to Niemeyer, 6 February, 1925.

159. *Ibid.*

160. The speech referred to appears in Midland Bank Limited, *Monthly Review*, January–February 1925, esp. 4–5.

161. T172/1499B, Churchill to Niemeyer, 6 February, 1925.

162. Chartwell Papers, File 18/10, Churchill to Chamberlain, 6 February, 1925.

163. T172/1499B, Niemeyer to Churchill.

164. T172/1499B, Chamberlain to Churchill, 8 February, 1925.

165. 8 February, 1925.

166. Leith-Ross, *op.cit.*, 91–2.

167. 21 February, 1925. It also appears in J.M. Keynes, *Essays in Persuasion*, (London, 1931), 225—36.

168. T172/1499B, Niemeyer to Churchill, 21 February, 1925; Keynes, *Essays*, 232.

169. *Ibid.*, 233—5.

170. *Ibid.*, 235.

171. T172/1499B, Churchill to Niemeyer, 22 February, 1925.

172. T172/1499B, Niemeyer to Churchill.

173. Above 48.

174. Grigg, *op.cit.*, 182—4. The date of the party is taken from Keynes' appointments diary for 1925 which is part of the Keynes Papers.

175. See for example T175/11, Churchill to Niemeyer, 20 April, 1927.

176. F.R.B.N.Y., Norman to Strong, No. 71, 24 February, 1925; Strong Papers, Norman to Strong, 9 March, 1925.

177. Boyle, *op.cit.*, 188—9. The quote given Boyle was also given the author by the late Mr. Churchill. See also 'Mr. Churchill's Success', *The Banker*, I(6), June 1926, 393.

178. Boyle, *op.cit.*, 189.

179. T172/1499B, Note by Niemeyer.

180. See 40.

181. T172/1500A, Norman to Niemeyer, 4 December, 1924.

182. T172/1500A, Niemeyer to Norman, 8 December, 1924.

183. T172/1500A, Fisher to Niemeyer, 12 January, 1925.

184. T175/9, Niemeyer to Lubbock, 9 January, 1925.

185. See above 43,44.

186. T172/1500A, Niemeyer to Phillips and Graham-Harrison, 22 January, 1925; Phillips to Graham-Harrison, 23 January, 1925; Graham-Harrison to Niemeyer, 24 January, 1925; Niemeyer to Norman, 25 January and 10 February, 1925; Norman to Niemeyer, 27 January, 10 and 26 February, 1925; Rowe-Dutton to Niemeyer, 19 February, 1925; Leith-Ross to Niemeyer, 13 March, 1925.

187. F.R.B.N.Y., Norman to Strong, No. 71, 23 February, 1925.

188. T172/1500A, Niemeyer to Norman, 16 March, 1925 and enclosure called 'The Cushion'.

189. *Ibid.* See also T172/1500A, Niemeyer to Churchill, 20 March, 1925.

190. Above 57.

191. T172/1500A, Norman to Strong, Nos. 87 and 88, 21 March, 1925.

192. T172/1500A, Strong to Norman, Nos. 48 and 49, 24 March, 1925; J.P. Morgan to E.C. Grenfell, No. 2076, 25 March, 1925.

193. T172/1500A, Norman to Strong, No. 91, 26 March, 1925.

194. T172/1500A, Norman to Strong, Nos. 91, 93 and 100, 25 and 30 March, and 2 April, 1925; Strong to Norman, Nos. 52,27 March, 1925; Niemeyer to Churchill, 30 March, 1925; Churchill to Niemeyer, 31 March, 1925; Norman to Niemeyer, 30 March, 1925.

195. T172/1500A, Norman to Strong, 8 April, 1925; T160/227/F8508, Churchill to J.P. Morgan and Co., 28 April, 1925; E.C. Grenfell and Co. to Churchill, 28 April, 1925.

196. F.R.B.N.Y., Strong Papers, Strong to Norman, 15 January, 1925.

197. F.R.B.N.Y., Strong Papers, Norman to Strong, 13 February, 1925.

198. T172/1499B, Niemeyer to Norman, 15 April, 1925.

199. T160/227/F8508, Treasury Minute, 14 May, 1925.

200. T172/1499/B, Norman to Niemeyer, 21 March, 1925.

201. T172/1500A, Niemeyer to Chancellor, Note on Norman's letter of 21 March, 1925.

202. T172/1500A, Norman to Strong, No. 92, 27 March, 1925.

203. *Ibid.*, T172/1500A, Norman to Niemeyer, 30 March, 1925; Strong to Norman, No. 53, 27 March, 1925.

204. Committee on the Currency and Bank of England Note Issues, *Report*, para. 34.

205. F.R.B.N.Y., Strong Papers, Strong to Norman, 30 April, 1925.

206. T176/22, Note of a Meeting between the Chancellor of the Exchequer and Representative's of the Clearing Banks, 23 March, 1925; Note of a second Meeting on 26 March, 1925 between the Chancellor of the Exchequer and the Bankers.

207. *Ibid.*, Niemeyer to Churchill, 25 February, 1925.

208. *Ibid.*, Niemeyer to Churchill, 6 April, 1925.

209. T176/22, R. Holland-Martin to Niemeyer, 23 April and 1 May, 1925.

210. Committee on the Currency and Bank of England Note Issues, *Report*, para. 45; T160/197/F7528, Niemeyer to Pigou 17 and 23 April, 1925; Gold Standard Act 1925, 15 and 16, Geo. 5, c. 29, Section 1.

211. Australia, New Zealand, the Netherlands, the Netherlands East Indies,

and South Africa agreed to move with England. Switzerland refused and wanted to wait until 'they have had time to witness the results of the action taken elsewhere, and particularly in Great Britain'. (Norman to Niemeyer, 20 April, 1925). The correspondence concerning the co-ordinating discussions appears in T172/1499B.

212. T160/197/F7528/01/1–3, Committee on the Currency and Bank of England Note Issues, Second Draft of Report, para. 5; Third Draft Report, para. 5; Fourth Draft Report, section 5; *Report*. para. 7.

213. Court of Inquiry concerning the Coal Mining Industry Dispute, 1925, *Report*, Cmd. 2478, (London, 1925), 21 ff.

214. T176/16, Niemeyer to Chancellor, 4 August, 1925; Bradbury, 'The Coal Crisis and the Gold Standard', 4 August, 1925. The Bradbury memo also appeared in the *Financial News*, 12 August, 1925.

215. *Report*, para. 8.

216. J.M. Keynes, 'Notes and Memoranda. The Committee on the Currency', 300.

217. T172/1499B, Bradbury, 'The Gold Standard', 5 February, 1925; Hawtrey, 'The Gold Standard', 2 February, 1925.

218. T172/1499B, Gold Standard Bill, Memorandum, 28 April, 1925, 5.

219. Particularly Bradbury, Hawtrey and Norman.

220. Grigg, *op.cit.*, 183.

221. T172/1499B, Niemeyer, 'The Gold Export Prohibition', 2 February, 1925; 'Commentary', 2 February, 1925; reply to Churchill's note of 22 February, 1925; 'Notes on Gold Standard', 29 April, 1925.

222. T172/1499B, Gold Standard Bill, Memorandum, 28 April, 1925, 5. A conference of Central Banks along the lines suggested at Genoa was under discussion at the time of the official decision to return to gold. T172/1499B, F.B.I. to Churchill, 17 March, 1925, 3; Niemeyer to Churchill, 20 March, 1925; T172/1500A, Norman to Strong, No. 87, 21 March, 1925; Strong to Norman, 48, 24 March, 1925. The proposal never came to anything.

223. On this point see Committee on Finance and Industry, *Evidence*, Question 6075, 6078.

224. See above 47, 49, 50, 52, 53.

225. R.Z. Aliber, 'Speculation in the Foreign Exchanges. The European Experience 1919–26', *Yale Economic Essays*, II(1), Spring 1962, esp. 194–7.

226. See below 74.

227. T176/16, Niemeyer to Churchill, 4 August, 1925; T172/1499B, Niemeyer, 'Commentary', 2 February, 1925; Niemeyer to Churchill, 6 February, 1925.

228. Committee on the Currency and Bank of England Note Issues, *Report*, para. 21. This represents a change from earlier drafts; for example the second — T160/197/F7528/01/2, Second Draft of Report, para. 19 (ii) and (iii). See also T160/463/F8362/1, Telegram, Governor General of Australia to Colonial Secretary, 8 January, 18 February and 10 March, 1925; Colonial Secretary to Governor General of Australia, 22 January, 27 February; T172/1499B, Telegram, S.M. Bruce to Baldwin, 9 April, 1925.

229. para. 19–20.

230. Pigou Papers, *op.cit.*, Evidence of Norman, June 1924, 19–20. See also Norman's January 1925 evidence to the Committee, 16; F.R.B.N.Y., Strong Papers, Norman to Strong, 16 October, 1924.

231. T172/1499B, Niemeyer, 'Notes on Gold Standard', 29 April, 1925; Bradbury, 'The Gold Standard', 5 February, 1925; Gold Standard Bill, Memorandum, 2–3. Committee on the Currency and Bank of England Note Issues, *Report*, para. 15.

232. Above 27, 28, 29, 34, 35, 37, 43, 44–5, 50.

233. See for example, Committee on the Currency and Bank of England Note Issues, *Report*, para. 15; Gold Standard Bill, Memorandum, 2–3.

234. J.M. Keynes, *Tract on Monetary Reform*, 91; *The Economic Consequences of Mr. Churchill*, 11.

235. Sayers, *op.cit.*, 320.

236. T172/1499B, Gold Standard Bill, Memorandum, 3–4.

237. T172/1499B, Bradbury, 'The Gold Standard', 5 February, 1925.

238. T172/1499B, Hawtrey, 'The Gold Standard', 2 February, 1925.

239. T172/1499B, Niemeyer, 'The Gold Export Prohibition',2 February, 1925, Section 7, Niemeyer to Churchill, 21 February, 1925; Norman to Churchill, 2 February, 1925, para. 3.

240. *Ibid.*, para. 7; Niemeyer, 'Notes on Gold Standard', 29 April, 1925.

241. T172/1499B, Norman to Churchill, 2 February, 1925, para. 5; F.R.B.N.Y., Norman to Strong, No. 71, 24 February, 1925; Strong Papers, Norman to Strong, 26 May, 1925.

242. T172/1499B, Niemeyer, 'The Gold Export Prohibition', 2 February, 1925, sections 6 and 11; 'Notes on Gold Standard', 29 April, 1925, section 7.

243. Grigg, *op.cit.*, 183.

244. Committee on the Currency and Bank of England Note Issues, *Report*, para. 32.

245. Grigg, *op.cit.*, 184.

246. Keynes Papers, Committee on Finance and Industry, Notes of Discussion, 23 October, 1930, 22.

247. See above

248. T175/16, Niemeyer to Churchill, 4 August, 1925, 5.

249. T176/16, Bradbury, 'The Coal Crisis and the Gold Standard', 4 August, 1925.

250. Pigou Papers, *op.cit.*, Evidence of J.M. Keynes, 14. The F.B.I. Statement also noted the effects on exports to the Chamberlain-Bradbury Committee, 3.

251. T172/1499B, Niemeyer, 'The Gold Export Prohibition', 2 February, 1925, Section 9; 'Notes on Gold Standard', 29 April, 1925; T176/16, Bradbury, 'The Coal Crisis and the Gold Standard', 4 August, 1925, 2.

252. T172/1499B, R.G. Hawtrey, 'Balance of Payments of the United Kingdom', undated.

253. Committee on the Currency and Bank of England Note Issues, *Report*, para. 12–13.

254. T172/1499B, Hawtrey, 'The Gold Standard and the Balance of Payments', 2 March, 1925 as amended by Niemeyer, 1–4; Niemeyer to Churchill, 10 March, 1925; Pigou Papers, *op.cit.*, Evidence of the Governor of the Bank of England and Sir Charles Addis, January 1925, 32.

255. T172/1499B, Hawtrey, 'The Gold Standard and the Balance of Payments', 2 March, 1925, 5–6; Pigou Papers, *op.cit.*, Evidence of the Governor of the Bank of England and Sir Charles Addis, 33–4; Committee on the Currency and Bank of England Note Issues, *Report*, para. 34–6; above pages 37, 44.

256. T172/1499B, Hawtrey, 'The Gold Standard and the Balance of Payments', 2 March, 1925, 7–8; Niemeyer to Churchill, 29 April, 1925; Pigou Papers, *op.cit.*, Evidence of the Governor of the Bank of England and Sir Charles Addis, 31.

257. *Ibid.*, 4–5.

258. For a good sample of opinion see the selections of contemporary clippings T172/1499B and T160/197/F7528/03.

259. Leith-Ross, *op.cit.*, 92.

260. T.E. Gregory, *The First Year of the Gold Standard*, (London, 1926), Ch. 1.

261. Hume, *op.cit.*, 242.

262. T172/1499B, R.T. Nugent to Churchill, 17 March, 1925.

263. See for example Grigg *op. cit.*, 193; Boyle, *op.cit.*, 190–91; Lord Moran, *The Struggle for Survival*, (London, 1966), 303–4.

264. C.P. Kindleberger, *Economic Growth in France and Britain 1860–1960*, (Cambridge, 1964), 266–7.

265. Committee on Finance and Industry, *Minutes of Evidence*, Q. 6075–6084.

266. Brown, *op.cit.*, 179.

Chapter III

1. J. Robinson, 'The Foreign Exchanges', *Essays in the Theory of Employment*, (London, 1937), 208.

2. B. Balassa and D.M. Schydlowsky, 'Effective Tariffs, Domestic Cost of Foreign Exchange, and the Equilibrium Exchange Rate', *Journal of Political Economy*, LXXVI (3) May/June, 1968, 357, 359.

3. W. Galenson and A. Zellner, 'International Comparison of Unemployment Rates', National Bureau of Economic Research, Special Conference Series *The Measurement and Behaviour of Unemployment*, (Princeton, 1957), Table 2, 459.

4. There are many additional examples to those in previously published sources. For readily available examples see Clay, *op.cit.*, 293–5.

5. See for example Keynes Papers, Committee on Finance and Industry, Notes of Discussions, 28 February, 1930, 4.

6. Cab. 58/9, Committee of Civil Research, Overseas Loans Sub-Committee, *Report*, 16 October, 1925. The membership of this sub-committee included Bradbury, Norman, J.C. Stamp, Niemeyer, S.J. Chapman, C.H. Kisch and Henry Lambert.

7. Keynes Papers, Committee on Finance and Industry, Notes of Discussions 7 November, 1930, 29.

8. T172/1499B, Niemeyer, 'The Gold Export Prohibition', 2 February, 1925, Section 9; Norman to Churchill, 2 February, 1925, para. 7; Hawtrey 'The Gold Standard', 2 February, 1925, 1–2, 9–10; Gold Standard Bill, Memorandum, 28 April, 1925, 4.

9. See above 17 ff.

10. W. Ashworth, *An Economic History of England 1870–1939* (London, 1960), 387; S. Pollard, *The Development of the British Economy 1914–1950*, (London, 1962), 217–20; C.P. Kindleberger, *op.cit.*, 207.

11. A.J. Youngson, *The British Economy 1920–1957*, (London, 1960), 230–38; Gregory, *op.cit.*, 53–4; Morgan, *op.cit.*, 367.

12. G. Haberler, *A Survey of International Trade Theory*, Special Papers in

International Economics, No. 1, rev. edn. (Princeton, 1961), 48.

13. J.M. Keynes, *A Treatise on Money*, I, (London, 1930), 67, 73.

14. *Ibid.*, 73–5; J.M. Keynes, *Tract on Monetary Reform*, 87–106.

15. Morgan, *op.cit.*, 361–7.

16. A. Maizels, *Industrial Growth and World Trade*, (Cambridge, 1963), 202–4.

17. This was the index used by Keynes, *The Economic Consequences of Mr. Churchill*, 11.

18. A.N. McLeod, 'A Critique of the Fluctuating-Exchange-Rate Policy in Canada', *The Bulletin*, No. 34–35, April–June, 1965, 62.

19. B. Balassa, 'The Purchasing-Power Parity Doctrine: A Reappraisal', *Journal of Political Economy*, LXXII (6), December, 1964, 593.

20. Haberler, *op.cit.*, 49–50.

21. *Ibid.*, 50.

22. Gregory, *op.cit.*, 51.

23. T179/1499B, Niemeyer, 'The Gold Export Prohibition', 2 February 1925, Section 9. The approach taken by Keynes to the French franc was a plausible means to stabilisation with important consequences for Britain; J.M. Keynes, 'An open letter to the French Minister of Finance (whoever he is or may be)', *Essays in Persuasion*, 105–113.

24. See, for example, Committee on Finance and Industry, *Minutes of Evidence*, Q. 3350 and following.

25. G.H. Orcutt, 'Measurements of Price Elasticities in International Trade', *The Review of Economics and Statistics*, XXXII(2), May 1950; F. Machlup, 'Elasticity Pessimism in International Trade', *Economica Internazionale*, III(1), February, 1950.

26. See for example, A.C. Harberger, 'Some Evidence on the International Price Mechanism', *Journal of Political Economy*, LXV (6), December 1957; R.E. Zelder, 'Estimates of Elasticities of Demand for Exports of the United Kingdom and the United States 1921–1938', *Manchester School*, XXVI(1), January 1958; A Maizels, *op.cit.*, 211–16; M.FG. Scott, *A Study of United Kingdom Imports*, (Cambridge, 1963), 49; and the literature cited therein.

27. A.S. Gerakis, 'Effects of Exchange-Rate Devaluations and Revaluations on Receipts from Tourism', *I.M.F. Staff Papers*, XII(3), November 1965.

28. Maizels, *op.cit.*, 217–24.

29. T172/1499B, Hawtrey, 'The Gold Standard', 2 February, 1925, 4–6. Here Hawtrey considers the possibilities of a fall in American prices resulting from credit contraction and argues that if this occurred the U.K. should be

prepared to let gold go and, if necessary, ultimately 'it would be better to let sterling relapse than to raise bank rate to a deterrent level'. However, such a development he considered unlikely.

30. Committee on Currency and Foreign Exchanges after the War, *First Interim Report*, para. 4–5; T172/1499B, R.G. Hawtrey, 'How does a gold standard work in regulating credit', undated.

31. Mitchell and Deane, *op.cit.*, Wages and Standard of Living 3.

32. Routh, *op.cit.*, 114.

33. *Ibid.*, 115.

34. A.G. Pool, *Wage Policy in Relation to Industrial Fluctuations*, (London, 1938), 256–7.

35. D.H. Aldcroft, 'Economic Growth in Britain in the Inter-War Years: A Reassessment', *Economic History Review*, 2nd series, XX(2), August 1967, 313–14; E.H. Phelps Brown and M.H. Browne, *A Century of Pay*, (London, 1968), Figure 36.

36. On the French revaluation see E. Moreau, *Souveniers d'un Gouverneur de la Banque de France*, (Paris, 1954), 177, 182–3.

37. Clay, *op.cit.*, 159.

Chapter IV

1. The first contemporary use of this phrase occurs in *The Nation*, 8 November, 1924, 230.

2. Keynes Papers, Committee on Finance and Industry, Notes of Discussions, 7, November, 1930, 24–25.

3. Svennilson, *op.cit.*, Table A3.

4. Brown and Browne, *op.cit.*, 229–32.

5. Maizels, *op.cit.*, Ch. VIII.

6. *Ibid.*, Table 8.1.

7. *Ibid.*, Table 8.4.

8. *Ibid.*, Table 8.5.

9. *Ibid.*, Table 8.6.

10. *Ibid.*, Table 8.13, 251.

11. *Ibid.*, Table 8.11.

12. See for example T.E. Gregory, *The Return to Gold*, (London, 1925), 52.

13. For a discussion of this unwillingness in a particular part of the period see

R. Skidelsky, *Politicians and the Slump*, (London, 1967).

14. O. Morgenstern, *International Financial Transactions and Business Cycles*, (Princeton, 1959), Table 40.

15. *Ibid.*, Charts 6, 56, 58, 62.

16. Brown, *op.cit.*, 709.

17. Both as a result of political pressures and of Treasury pressures. For the latter, Clay, *op.cit.*, 293–97, gives some clues as to the position, but does not indicate the almost continuous Treasury pressure for an easier monetary policy, particularly under Churchill. This pressure can be best seen in T176/13.

18. Scattered accounts of various developments exist in Clay, *op.cit.*, especially Chapters VI and VII. This study is a part of a larger effort that will pay specific attention to the development of techniques in this area.

19. The distinction between correction and adjustment has been developed by Professor Machlup. See F. Machlup, 'In Search of Guides for Policy', W. Fellner, F. Machlup, R. Triffin *et al.*, *Maintaining and Restoring Balance in International Payments*, (Princeton, 1966), esp. 50–63.

20. J.M. Keynes, 'Our Monetary Policy', *Financial News*, 18 August, 1925.

21. Cab. 58/9, Committee of Civil Research, Overseas Loans Sub-Committee *Report*; Committee on Finance and Industry, *Report*, 263–81; T175/56, H.A. Siepmann, Note of a Conversation with Lord Bradbury, 24 September, 1931.

22. Above 28, 48, 49.

23. See *The Nation*, 2 May, 1925; letter to *The Times*, 6 May, 1925.

24. J.M. Keynes, *The Economic Consequences of Mr. Churchill*, 27.

25. J.M. Keynes, 'Discussion on Monetary Reform', *Economic Journal*, XXXIV (134), June 1924, 174.

26. J.M. Keynes, letter to *The Times*, 20 March, 1925.

27. See above 28, 47, 48.

28. See above 9; Keynes Papers, Committee on Finance and Industry, Notes of Discussions, 7 November, 1930, 15 ff.

29. See, for example, Cab. 58/9, Committee of Civil Research, Overseas Loans Sub-Committee, *Report*, para. 28, 30.

30. Young, *op.cit.*, 234, Clay, *op.cit.*, 169–71.

31. D. Williams, 'The Evolution of the Sterling System', C.R. Whittlesey and J.S.G. Wilson, *Essays in Money and Banking in Honour of R.S. Sayers*, (Oxford, 1968), 266.

32. What follows depends heavily on A.K. Swoboda, 'The Euro-Dollar Market: An Interpretation', *Essays in International Finance*, No.64, February, 1968, 5–11, 39–41.

33. W. Baumol, 'The Transactions Demand for Cash: An Inventory Theoretic Approach', *Quarterly Journal of Economics*, LXVI(4), November 1952; J. Tobin, 'The Interest Elasticity of the Transactions Demand for Cash', *Review of Economics and Statistics*, XXXVIII(3), August, 1956.

34. Above 76–7.

35. Above 54.

36. Above 31–2; 'F.B.I. and Currency Policy: A Restatement', *Manchester Guardian Commercial*, 29 October, 1925.

37. Sayers, *op.cit.*, 316.

38. Above 32; T172/1499B, R.G. Glenday to Churchill, 17 March, 1925, 3.

39. Sayers, *op.cit.*, 316.

40. Committee on Finance and Industry, *Minutes of Evidence*, Q6089–97.

41. *Ibid.*, Q6089; Youngson, *op.cit.*, 237; Sayers, *op.cit.*, 321.

42. This point is developed by Professor Sayers, *op.cit.*, 324 ff.

43. See for example, O.E. Niemeyer, 'How to Economize Gold', Royal Institute of International Affairs, *The International Gold Problem*, (London 1931), 90–91.

44. For an introduction to the proposal, Clarke, *op.cit.*, 179–81; Skidelsky, *op.cit.*, 285–6.

45. G. Myrdal, *An International Economy*, (New York, 1956), 72–3.

46. Cab. 58/11, The State of Trade, Answers by Mr. Keynes, 21 July, 1930.

Appendix

1. A.C. Harberger, *op.cit.*; R.E. Zelder, *op.cit.*, A. Maizels, *op.cit.*, 211–216; M.FG. Scott, *op.cit.*; A.J. Brown, 'The Fundamental Elasticities in International Trade', T. Wilson and P.W.S. Andrews eds., *Oxford Studies in the Price Mechanism*, (Oxford, 1951); Z. Kubinski, 'The Elasticity of Substitution between Sources of British Imports 1921–1938', *Yorkshire Bulletin of Economic and Social Research*, II(1), January 1950; G.D.A. MacDougall, 'British and American Exports: A Study Suggested by the Theory of Comparative Costs', *Economic Journal* LXI (244) and LXII (247), December 1951 and September 1952.

2. Royal Institute of International Affairs, *The Problem of International Investment*, (London, 1937), 148, 150, 152.

3. Brown and Browne, *op.cit.*, Appendix III.

4. T.C. Chang, *Cyclical Movements in the Balance of Payments*, (Cambridge, 1951), Ch. VI.

5. Brown and Browne, *op.cit.*, Appendix III.